SRA ART Connections

Level 4

Authors

Rosalind Ragans, Ph.D., Senior Author

Willis "Bing" Davis   Jane Rhoades Hudak, Ph.D.   Bunyan Morris
Tina Farrell   Gloria McCoy   Nan Yoshida

Contributing Author

Jackie Ellett

ART
SOU
RCE
ARTSOURCE

Education Division
The Music Center of Los Angeles County

SRA

Columbus, OH

The McGraw-Hill Companies

Authors

Senior Author
Dr. Rosalind Ragans, Ph.D.
Associate Professor Emerita
Georgia Southern University

Willis "Bing" Davis
Associate Professor Emeritus
Central State University - Ohio
President & Founder of
SHANGO: The Center for the
Study of African American
Art & Culture

Tina Farrell
Assistant Superintendent
Curriculum and Instruction
Clear Creek Independent
School District,
League City, Texas

Jane Rhoades Hudak, Ph.D.
Professor of Art
Georgia Southern University

Gloria McCoy
Former President
Texas Art Education Association
Spring Branch Independent
School District, Texas

Bunyan Morris
Art Teacher
Effingham County School
System, Springfield, Georgia

Nan Yoshida
Art Education Consultant
Retired Art Supervisor
Los Angeles Unified School
District
Los Angeles, California

SRAonline.com

 **SRA**

Send all inquiries to:
SRA/McGraw-Hill
8787 Orion Place
Columbus, OH 43240-4027

Printed in the United States of America.

ISBN 0-07-601823-7

3 4 5 6 7 8 9 RRW 10 09 08 07 06 05

The McGraw-Hill Companies

Contributors

Contributing Author
Jackie Ellett, Ed. S.
Elementary Art Teacher
Duncan Creek Elementary School
Hoschton, Georgia

Contributing Writer
Lynda Kerr, NBCT
Ed.D. Candidate, Art Teacher
Henry County, Georgia

Artsource® Music, Dance, Theatre Lessons
Mark Slavkin, Vice President
for Education, The Music Center of
Los Angeles County
Michael Solomon, Managing Director
Music Center Education Division
Melinda Williams, Concept Originator and
Project Director
Susan Cambigue-Tracey, Project Coordinator

and Writer
Madeleine Dahm, Movement and Dance
Connection Writer
Keith Wyffels, Staff Assistance
Maureen Erbe, Logo Design

More about Aesthetics
Richard W. Burrows
Executive Director, Institute for Arts
Education
San Diego, California

Safe Use of Art Materials
Mary Ann Boykin
Director, The Art School for Children and
Young Adults
University of Houston—Clear Lake
Houston, Texas

Museum Education
Marilyn J. S. Goodman
Director of Education
Solomon R. Guggenheim Museum
New York, New York

Resources for Students with Disabilities
Mandy Yeager
Ph.D. Candidate
The University of North Texas
Denton, Texas

Music Connections
Kathy Mitchell
Music Teacher
Eagan, Minnesota

Student Activities

Cassie Appleby
Glen Oaks Elementary School
McKinney, Texas

Maureen Banks
Kester Magnet School
Van Nuys, California

Christina Barnes
Webb Bridge Middle School
Alpharetta, Georgia

Beth Benning
Willis Jepson Middle School
Vacaville, California

Chad Buice
Craig Elementary School
Snellville, Georgia

Beverly Broughton
Gwinn Oaks Elementary School
Snellville, Georgia

Missy Burgess
Jefferson Elementary School
Jefferson, Georgia

Marcy Cincotta-Smith
Benefield Elementary School
Lawrenceville, Georgia

Joanne Cox
Kittredge Magnet School
Atlanta, Georgia

Carolyn Y. Craine
McCracken County Schools
Paducah, Kentucky

Jackie Ellett
Duncan Creek Elementary School
Hoschton, Georgia

Tracie Flynn
Home School
Rushville, Indiana

Phyllis Glenn
Malcom Bridge Elementary
Bogart, Georgia

Dallas Gillespie
Dacula Middle School
Dacula, Georgia

Dr. Donald Gruber
Clinton Junior High School
Clinton, Illinois

Karen Heid
Rock Springs Elementary School
Lawrenceville, Georgia

Alisa Hyde
Southwest Elementary
Savannah, Georgia

Kie Johnson
Oconee Primary School
Watkinsville, Georgia

Sallie Keith, NBCT
West Side Magnet School
LaGrange, Georgia

Letha Kelly
Grayson Elementary School
Grayson, Georgia

Diana Kimura
Amestoy Elementary School
Gardena, California

Desiree LaOrange
Barkley Elementary School
Fort Campbell, Kentucky

Deborah Lackey-Wilson
Roswell North Elementary
Roswell, Georgia

Dawn Laird
Goforth Elementary School
Clear Creek, Texas

Mary Lazzari
Timothy Road Elementary School
Athens, Georgia

Michelle Leonard
Webb Bridge Middle School
Alpharetta, Georgia

Lynn Ludlam
Spring Branch ISD
Houston, Texas

Mark Mitchell
Fort Daniel Elementary School
Dacula, Georgia

Martha Moore
Freeman's Mill Elementary School
Dacula, Georgia

Connie Niedenthal
Rushville Elementary
Rushville, Indiana

Barbara Patisaul
Oconee County Elementary
School
Watkinsville, Georgia

Elizabeth Paulos-Krasle
Social Circle Elementary
Social Circle, Georgia

Jane Pinneau
Rocky Branch Elementary School
Watkinsville, Georgia

Marilyn Polin
Cutler Ridge Middle School
Miami, Florida

Michael Ramsey
Graves County Schools
Mayfield, Kentucky

Rosemarie Sells
Social Circle Elementary
Social Circle, Georgia

Jean Neelen–Siegel
Baldwin School
Alhambra, California

Debra Smith
McIntosh County School System
Darien, Georgia

Patricia Spencer
Harmony Elementary School
Buford, Georgia

Melanie Stokes
Smiley Elementary School
Ludowici, Georgia

Rosanne Stutts
Davidson Fine Arts School
Augusta, Georgia

Fran Sullivan
South Jackson Elementary School
Athens, Georgia

Kathy Valentine
Home School
Burkburnett, Texas

Debi West
Rock Springs Elementary School
Lawrenceville, Georgia

Sherry White
Bauerschlag Elementary School
League City, Texas

Patricia Wiesen
Cutler Ridge Middle School
Miami, Florida

Deayna Woodruff
Loveland Middle School
Loveland, Ohio

Gil Young
El Rodeo School
Beverly Hills, California

Larry A. Young
Dacula Elementary School
Dacula, Georgia

Table of Contents

What Is Art?

About Art

◀ **Natalia Goncharova.**
Maquillage.

Unit 1 Line

▲ **Stuart Davis.**
Composition.

Unit 2 Shape, Pattern, Rhythm, and Movement

◄ **Miriam Schapiro.**
Pas de Deux.

Unit 3 Color and Value

◀ **Michelangelo.**
Pietà.

Unit 4 Form, Texture, and Emphasis

▲ **John Singelton Copley.**
Sir William Pepperrell and His Family.

Unit 5 Space, Proportion, and Distortion

▲ **Judith Leyster.**
The Concert.

Unit 6 Balance, Harmony, Variety, and Unity

Technique Tips

Activity Tips

Visual Index

What Is Art?

Art is . . .

Painting is color applied to a flat surface.

▲ **Vincent Van Gogh.** (French). *Houses at Auvers.* 1890.

Oil on canvas. $29\frac{3}{4} \times 24\frac{3}{8}$ inches (75.56 × 61.93 cm.). Museum of Fine Arts, Boston, Massachusetts.

Drawing is the process of making art with lines.

▲ **Pablo Picasso.** (Spanish). *Portrait of Dora Maar.* 1938.

Pencil on paper mounted on fiberboard. $30\frac{9}{16} \times 22\frac{7}{16}$ inches (77.62 × 57 cm.). Hirshhorn Museum and Sculpture Garden, Smithsonian Institution, Washington, D.C.

Sculpture is art that fills up space.

▲ **David Bates.** (American). *Seated Man #4.* 1995.

Painted wood. $88 \times 37\frac{1}{2} \times 45\frac{1}{2}$ inches (223.52 × 95.25 × 115.57 cm.). Dallas Museum of Art, Dallas, Texas.

Architecture is the art of designing and constructing buildings.

▲ **Jørn Oberg Utzon.** (Danish). *Opera House.* 1957–1973.

Sydney, Australia.

Printmaking is the process of transferring an original image from one prepared surface to another.

▲ **Katsushika Hokusai.** (Japanese.) *Winter Loneliness,* from *One Hundred Poems Explained by the Nurse.* 1839.
....
Woodcut. $10\frac{1}{16} \times 14\frac{1}{2}$ inches (25.5 × 36.8 cm.). Honolulu Academy of Art, Honolulu, Hawaii

Ceramics is the art of making objects with clay.

▲ **Artist Unknown.** (Kongo peoples, Congo and Democratic Republic of Congo.) **Bowl.** Late-nineteenth to early-twentieth century.
....
Ceramic and resin. $5\frac{7}{8} \times 4\frac{1}{8} \times 5\frac{7}{8}$ inches (14.9 × 10.49 × 14.94 cm.). National Museum of African Art, Smithsonian Institution, Washington, D.C.

Photography is the act of capturing an image on film.

◄ **Eliot Elisofon.** (American). *Asante Paramount Chief Nana Akyanfuo Akowuah Dateh II, Akwamuhene of Kumase.* 1970.
....
Photograph. National Museum of African Art, Smithsonian Institution, Washington, D.C.

A mask is a covering for the face to be used in ceremonies and other events.

▲ **Charlie James.** (Southern Kwakiutl.) *Sun Tranformation Mask.* Early nineteenth century.
....
Royal British Columbia Museum, British Columbia, Canada.

Art is created by people

► to communicate ideas.

► to express feelings.

► to give us well-designed objects.

What Is Art?

Every work of art has three parts.

Subject

The objects you can recognize are the subject matter of a work of art. When a work has no recognizable objects, the elements of art such as lines, shapes, colors, and so on become the subject of the work.

Composition

The composition of the work is the way the artist has used the principles to organize the elements of art.

Content

The content is the message the artwork communicates. Content is the meaning of the work. If the work is functional, such as a chair or clothing, then the content is the function of the object.

▶ In which work of art do you think the subject matter is very important?

▶ In which artwork do you think composition is most important?

▶ Which work seems to have the strongest message? Explain.

▶ Which artwork's meaning relates to its function?

▲ **William Sharp.** (English/American). *Great Water Lily of America.* 1854.

Chromolithograph on woven white paper. $21\frac{1}{4} \times 27$ inches (53.98 × 68.58 cm.). Amon Carter Museum, Fort Worth, Texas.

▲ **Benny Andrews.** (American). *Grandmother's Dinner.* 1992.

Oil on canvas. 72 × 52 inches (182.88 × 132.08 cm.). Ogden Museum of Southern Art, New Orleans, Louisiana.

▲ **Mosche Safdie.** (Israeli). *Habitat.* 1967.

Concrete. Montreal, Canada.

▲ **Artist Unknown.** (Maya/Huipil). *Huipil Weaving.* c. 1950.

Backstrap woven plain weave with supplementary-weft pattern, silk on cotton. 50 × $14\frac{1}{2}$ inches (127 × 36.83 cm.). Museum of International Folk Art, Santa Fe, New Mexico.

What Is Art?

Subject Matter

Artists make art about many subjects. *Subject matter* is the content of an artist's work. For example, the subject of a painting can be a vase of flowers or a self-portrait. This subject matter is easy to see. The subject matter is harder to understand when the artwork stands for something beyond itself. Look at the artwork on these pages. Notice the different kinds of subject matter.

Still Life

▲ **Paul Cézanne.** (French). *Still Life with Basket of Apples.* 1895.

Oil on canvas. $23\frac{3}{5} \times 31\frac{1}{2}$ inches (60 × 80 cm.). The Art Institute of Chicago, Chicago, Illinois.

Landscape

▲ **Z. Vanessa Helder.** (American). *Rocks and Concrete.* c. 1940.

Watercolor on paper. 19 × 15⅞ inches (48.26 × 40.34 cm.). Cheney Cowles Museum, Spokane, Washington.

What Is Art?

Genre

▲ **Winslow Homer.** (American.) *Nooning.* c. 1872.

Oil on canvas. $13\frac{5}{16} \times 19\frac{5}{8}$ inches (33.02 × 48.26 cm.). Wadsworth Atheneum, Hartford, Connecticut.

Nonobjective

◀ **Natalya Goncharova.** (Russian). *Maquillage.* 1913.
Gouache on paper. $4\frac{3}{8} \times 6\frac{3}{8}$ inches (11.13 × 16.21 cm.). Dallas Museum of Art, Dallas, Texas.

Portrait

◀ **Elizabeth Catlett.** (American). *Sharecropper.* 1970.
Color linocut. 26 × 22 inches (66.04 × 55.88 cm.). Smithsonian American Art Museum, Washington, D.C.

What Is Art?

Allegory

▲ **Jan van Eyck.** (Flemish.) *Portrait of Giovanni Arnolfini and His wife Giovanna Cenami.* 1434.

Oil on wood panel. 32 x 23 inches. The National Gallery, London, England.

Symbolism

▲ **Artist Unknown.** (Huichol People/Mexico). *Mother of the Eagles.* 1991.

Braided yarn embedded in vegetable wax on wood. $15\frac{3}{4} \times 19\frac{1}{2}$ inches (40 × 49.53 cm.). Private collection.

What Is Art?

Elements of Art

Art is a language. The words of the language are the elements of art.

Principles of Art

Artists organize their artwork using the principles of art.

Pattern

Rhythm

Balance

Emphasis

Harmony

Variety

Unity

About Art

▲ **Frida Kahlo.** (Mexican). *Frida y Diego Rivera.* 1931.

....

Oil on canvas. 39⅜ × 31 inches (100.01 × 78.74 cm.). San Francisco Museum of Modern Art, San Francisco, California.

Art History and Culture

Look at the artwork.

▶ What people or objects do you see?

▶ Do they look like people and objects you see around you today? Explain.

Look at the caption.

▶ When was the artwork created?

▶ What can you learn about the artist?

Learn more.

▶ Do some research to find out more about the artist, the artwork, and the time period.

About Art

▲ **Frida Kahlo.** (Mexican). *Frida y Diego Rivera.* 1931.

Oil on canvas. 39⅜ × 31 inches (100.01 × 78.74 cm.). San Francisco Museum of Modern Art, San Francisco, California.

Look

▶ Look at the work of art. What sounds, smells, or feelings are in this work of art?

▶ What happened just before and just after in this work of art?

▶ What kind of music would be playing in this work of art?

Look Inside

▶ Imagine you are one of these people. Who are you? What are you thinking? How do you feel?

▶ If you could add yourself to the painting, what would you look like? What would you be doing?

▶ Act out or tell the story in this work of art with a beginning, a middle, and an end.

▶ Draw what you can't see in this work of art. Are there hidden images that should be revealed?

Look Outside

▶ How is this like or different from your own world?

▶ What does the artist want you to know or think about in this work of art?

▶ Describe your journey in viewing this work of art. Include your thoughts, ideas, and changes in thinking.

▶ What will you remember about this work?

About Art

▲ **Frida Kahlo.** (Mexican). *Frida y Diego Rivera.* 1931.

Oil on canvas. 39⅜ × 31 inches (100.01 × 78.74 cm.). San Francisco Museum of Modern Art, San Francisco, California.

Describe

▶ List everything you see in this painting. Be sure to describe the people and their clothing.

Analyze

▶ How has the artist used line, shape, color, value, space, and texture?

▶ What kind of balance has the artist used?

▶ Has the artist used emphasis to make us notice one thing more than others?

Interpret

▶ What is happening?

▶ What is the artist telling us about these two people?

Decide

▶ Have you ever seen another artwork like this?

▶ Is it successful because it is realistic?

▶ Is it successful because it is well-organized?

▶ Is it successful because you have strong feelings when you study it?

About Art

▲ **Frida Kahlo.** (Mexican). *Frida y Diego Rivera.* 1931.
....
Oil on canvas. 39⅜ × 31 inches (100.01 × 78.74 cm.). San Francisco Museum of Modern Art, San Francisco, California.

How does an artist create a work of art?

Art is a process. You can follow the same steps to create your own work of art.

1. Get an idea.

▶ Artists get inspiration from many places. Look around you. People, objects, and scenes may provide inspiration for a work of art.

2. Plan your work.

▶ Do you want your artwork to be two-dimensional or three-dimensional?

▶ Decide what media you want to use.

▶ What materials will you need?

3. Make a sketch.

▶ Think about how you want your artwork to look. Sketch several ideas.

▶ If your artwork will be three-dimensional, sketch it from different points of view.

▶ Then choose the best idea.

4. Use the media.

▶ Make an artwork based on your best idea. You may want to practice using the materials first.

▶ When making your composition, remember the elements and principles of art. How can you use them to make your artwork say what you want it to say?

5. Share your final work.

▶ Evaluate your work using the four steps of art criticism. What do you like best about your work? What would you do differently next time?

Safety

▶ Use art materials only on your artwork.

▶ Keep art materials out of your mouth, eyes and ears.

▶ Use scissors and other sharp tools carefully. Keep your fingers away from the cutting blades.

▶ Wash your hands after using the art materials.

▶ Wear an art shirt or smock to protect your clothes.

▶ Use only art materials with a "nontoxic" label.

- ▶ Return art materials to their proper storage place.
- ▶ Be careful not to breathe chalk or clay dust.
- ▶ Use only new and clean foam trays.
- ▶ Do not walk around the room with sharp tools in your hand.
- ▶ Be aware of others in your work space.
- ▶ Always follow your teacher's directions when using the art materials.

Line

◀ **Natalya Goncharova.**
(Russian). *Maquillage.* 1913.

Gouache on paper. $4\frac{3}{8} \times 6\frac{3}{8}$ inches
(11.13 × 16.21 cm.). Dallas Museum
of Art, Dallas, Texas.

Artists use a variety of lines to create artwork.

Maquillage is a nonobjective painting by
Natalya Goncharova. She used a variety of lines
in this painting. In French, the word *maquillage*
refers to makeup. This may be a clue to the
meaning of this painting.

Artists use **lines** in drawings, paintings, and sculptures to create shapes and movement.

▶ What types of lines do you see in the painting by Natalya Goncharova?

▶ What type of line do you see more than once?

▶ Does this painting seem like a close-up or a faraway view?

▶ What do the lines in the center of the painting indicate?

In This Unit you will learn about and practice techniques used to create lines in artwork.

Here are the topics you will study:
▶ Types of Lines
▶ Gesture Drawing
▶ Observation Drawing
▶ Contour Lines
▶ Flowing Lines
▶ Shading Techniques

Self Portrait with Yellow Lilies

Natalya Goncharova
(1881–1962)

Natalya Goncharova was born in central Russia. She studied sculpture at the Moscow School of Painting, Sculpture, and Architecture. After her studies, Goncharova devoted her full attention to painting. She was one of a group of artists who led the movement from traditional to nonobjective art in Russia. In 1917 Goncharova settled permanently in Paris, where she designed for the theater and continued to paint until the end of her life.

Types of Lines

▲ **Jaune Quick-to-See Smith.**
(American). *Rainbow.* 1989.
. . . .
Oil and mixed-media on canvas.
66 × 84 inches (167.64 × 213.36 cm.).
Private Collection.

Look at the art on these pages. Jaune Quick-to-See Smith created her painting using loose brushstrokes to reflect her feelings about the environment. The symbols in her painting are similar to symbols in ancient Native American petroglyphs (rock drawings). Kandinsky's painting is nonobjective: it has no subject matter. Kandinsky painted colors and shapes as his subjects, which expressed his feelings.

Art History and Culture

How can you tell when an artwork has a subject matter, such as Smith's painting, or no subject matter, such as Kandinsky's painting?

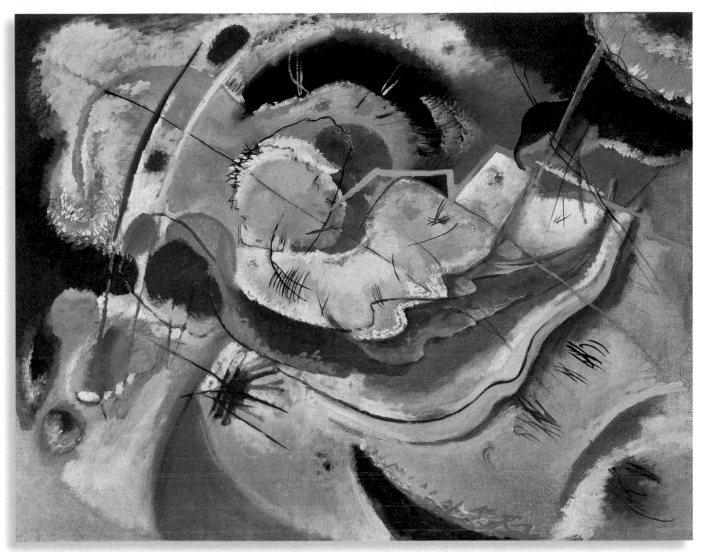

▲ **Wassily Kandinsky.** (Russian).
*Little Painting with Yellow
(Improvisation).* 1914.
. . . .
Oil on canvas. 31 × 39$\frac{5}{8}$ inches
(78.74 × 100.64 cm.). Philadelphia Museum
of Art, Philadelphia, Pennsylvania.

Study both works of art to find the different types
of lines.

▶ Identify line directions.

▶ Look for thick and thin lines.

▶ Where do you see rough and smooth lines?

▶ Can you find broken and solid lines?

Aesthetic Perception

Design Awareness Think of line designs on clothing, or look for
various line designs on objects in the room.

Using Lines

A **line** is a mark drawn by a tool such as a pencil, pen, or paintbrush as it moves across a surface. Artists use lines to define how an object looks.

Here are some different types of lines:

A **vertical line** moves up and down.

A **horizontal line** moves from side to side or from left to right.

A **diagonal line** is slanted.

Zigzag lines are diagonal lines that connect.

Curved lines bend and change direction slowly.

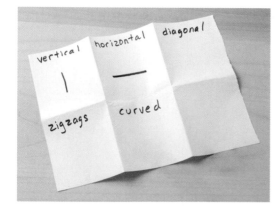

Practice

Draw each line and its variation. Use markers.

1. Fold a sheet of paper into six equal boxes. Print the name of each of the five types of lines at the top of each box, leaving one box empty.

2. Using a black marker, create the type of line indicated.

3. In the empty box, create a design using all five types of lines.

◀ **Christopher Cornelison.**
Age 8.

Think about what kinds of lines the student artist used in the poster.

🎨 Creative Expression

What emotions do you feel when you think about a cause that concerns you? Create a poster. Use different kinds of lines and a slogan to represent your cause.

1. Think about a cause that concerns you, such as pollution. Write a short slogan or message that expresses your concerns.

2. Design a poster about your cause. Use the different kinds of lines and line variations that you saw in the artwork. Plan a way to work your slogan into a design, like Jaune Quick-to-See Smith did.

⚠️❓ Art Criticism

Describe Name the objects and the slogan in your poster.

Analyze List the different lines you used. How did you make your slogan fit the design?

Interpret Does your poster express your concerns? Do your friends understand what you are trying to say?

Decide Did you use the five different kinds of lines in your poster? Explain.

Gesture Drawings

Look at the works of art on these two pages. *Self-Portrait (the Memory)* was painted by Audrey Flack in 1958, when she was an art student. *Sheet of Studies for "The Martyrdom of Saint George"* was created in Italy around 1566. It is a full page of gesture sketches used as a study for a painting. Artists make many studies of models before they begin their final compositions.

◄ **Audrey Flack.** (American).
Self-Portrait (the Memory). 1958.

Oil on canvas. 50 × 34 inches (127 × 86.36 cm.). Art Museum of Miami University, Oxford, Ohio.

Art History and Culture

Notice the nationality of each artist and the year each artwork was created. How would Flack's self-portrait be different if she had been a woman living in the sixteenth century?

▲ **Paolo Veronese.** (Italian). *Sheet of Studies for "The Martyrdom of Saint George."* c. 1566.

Pen and brown ink and brown wash. $11\frac{3}{8} \times 8\frac{9}{16}$ inches (28.9 × 21.7 cm.). J. Paul Getty Museum, Los Angeles, California.

Study both works of art and find the lines that show movement.

► Find a repeated line that represents movement.

► Which figure seems to be the most lively? Which figure seems to be the calmest?

► Describe how detail is used or not used in each work of art.

► Compare the works of art. What similarities do you see? What differences do you see?

Aesthetic Perception

Seeing Like an Artist Look around the classroom. Observe how everyone is moving. Notice the variety of gestures around you. What do these gestures represent?

Using Gesture Drawings

A **gesture** is an expressive movement. **Gesture lines** are quickly drawn to capture the movement of a person, an animal, or an object in a painting or drawing.

A **gesture sketch** is a quick sketch. To capture the gesture of an object, quick sketches or action drawings are used. The idea is to capture the movement or action of the object.

Repeated lines are used to give the feeling of movement or motion.

Repeated shapes, like hands or legs, also give the feeling of motion. The more times that shapes are repeated, the faster the motion looks.

Because gesture lines are used to capture movement, **minimal details** are used in the rest of the drawing. Often details are only suggested; for example, a few lines can suggest a mouth or an eye.

Practice

Illustrate the three gesture techniques. Use crayon.

1. Make quick sketches capturing the gestures of several of your classmates.

2. Make sure your sketches have repeated lines, shapes, and very little detail.

◄ **Hayden Verner.**
Age 9.

Think about how the student artist created the feeling of movement in the drawing.

Creative Expression

How can you capture the look of movement in a drawing? Create the feeling of movement in a gesture drawing.

1. Think about how action is captured in a drawing. Use quick, sketchy lines.

2. Take turns with classmates freezing in a movement. Hold poses for 30 seconds. Each time you draw someone new, change the crayon color.

3. Repeat lines and shapes and let your figures overlap to fill the entire page.

Art Criticism

Describe Describe the figures in your drawing.

Analyze Talk about the various gesture techniques that you used.

Interpret What type of feeling have you created in your drawing? What kinds of lines seem to represent action?

Decide Do you feel that you successfully caught the gestures of your classmates? Explain.

Observation Drawings

▲ **Pieter Bruegel the Elder.** (Flemish). *Children's Games.* 1560.

Oil on oakwood panel. $46\frac{1}{2} \times 63\frac{3}{8}$ inches (118.11 × 160.99 cm.). Kunsthistorisches Museum, Gemaldegalerie, Vienna, Austria.

Look at the paintings on these pages. *Children's Games* shows children in the sixteenth century playing games. At least 80 games are portrayed in this painting. *Endangered Species* by Paul Goodnight also focuses on children. However, they are in a completely different environment. Both *Children's Games* and *Endangered Species* are genre paintings, showing everyday life.

Art History and Culture

Notice the title of each artwork and the movement of the children. Use descriptive words to compare the environments portrayed in each painting.

▲ **Paul Goodnight.**
(American). *Endangered Species.* c. 1970.
....
Acrylic. $2\frac{1}{2}$ × 5 feet (.76 × 1.52 meters).
Private collection.

Study both works of art and notice how they show different ways of seeing action.

▶ What point of view did each artist use?

▶ How many different games can you find in Bruegel's painting?

▶ Both artists portrayed children moving very differently in their environments. What different messages do you think the artists were sending? What feelings do you get when you look at each painting?

Aesthetic Perception

Design Awareness Look around the room at your classmates. How do the students close to you look in relation to students right behind them and to those even farther away?

Using Observation Drawings

An observation drawing is a drawing made while looking at a person or object. Artists draw figures or objects in relation to their surroundings, but a painting can often show different points of view.

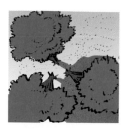

In a **bird's-eye view or aerial view** viewers feel they are looking down on a scene.

In an **ant's view** viewers feel they are looking up, toward an object or figure.

In a **faraway or eye-level view** viewers feel they are standing far away from the scene.

In a **close-up view** viewers feel they are right next to an object, or are a part of the action in a picture.

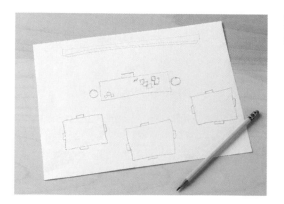

Practice

Create an observation drawing. Use pencil.

1. Draw a scene from the room. Use one of the points of view listed above.
2. Look at the points of view in *Children's Games* and *Endangered Species* for ideas.

Think about how the student artist created the observation drawing.

Creative Expression

How can you best capture the action of a group of children running and playing? Draw a sketch by observing children at play.

1. Think about repeating lines and shapes to draw gestures.

2. Go to the school playground and watch all the action that is taking place.

3. Sketch a variety of gestures from a specific point of view. Show the gestures of the children and some of their environment. Fill the entire page. Be sure to overlap your objects and use a variety of lines.

Art Criticism

Describe Describe the children and their environment.

Analyze Explain how you captured the children's gestures in relation to their environment.

Interpret Decide how your selected viewpoint creates a certain feeling in your picture.

Decide Did you successfully draw the gestures of the children in relation to their environment? Explain.

Contour Lines

Look at the works of art on these pages. Matisse made this pen-and-ink drawing in 1939. His drawing is a portrait. Andrews's drawing is a reflection of his experiences with everyday people. His drawing is a narrative. Notice how both artists used contour lines to define the edges and ridges of the subjects in their drawings.

◀ **Benny Andrews.** (American). *Patriots.* 1991.

Pen and ink on paper. $22\frac{1}{2}$ × 15 inches (57.15 × 38.1 cm.). Cumberland Gallery, Nashville, Tennessee.

Art History and Culture

Notice the years that the works of art were created. *Patriots* is considered a contemporary work of art. What does *contemporary* mean?

Study both works of art to see how lines flow throughout them.

► Describe some of the lines you see.

► What areas are emphasized more than others? What techniques did the artists use to emphasize these areas?

► Think of three adjectives to describe the couple in Andrews's drawing. Then list three adjectives to describe Matisse's woman.

▲ **Henri Matisse.** (French). *Portrait of a Woman with a Hood.* 1939.

Lead pencil. $13\frac{1}{16} \times 10\frac{1}{16}$ inches (33.2 × 25.6 cm.). State Hermitage Museum, St. Petersburg, Russia.

Aesthetic Perception

Design Awareness Closely observe objects in your environment. Notice changes in surface areas that would be defined as contours in a drawing.

Using Contour Lines

The **contour** of an object or figure is its edges and surface ridges. Artists often make contour drawings of objects and use them as studies before making a painting or drawing. Artists also make blind contour drawings, which help them to become more perceptive. Even if these drawings are not very accurate, making them develops an artist's ability to observe.

Contour lines are lines that show the edges and surface ridges of an object.

A **blind contour drawing** is a drawing that is made by looking at the object being drawn, not at the paper. You make a blind contour drawing by following the edges and ridges of an object with your eyes as you slowly draw it with your pen. Try not to look at your paper; instead, concentrate on the object you are drawing. Do not lift your pen from the paper. Try to draw one continuous line

Practice

Create a blind contour drawing of your hand. Use a felt-tip pen.

1. Look closely at your hand. Notice all the contours, the outer edges, the folds where you close your hand, and the lines around your knuckles.

2. Draw a blind contour of your hand, looking at it from one angle. Try to make your drawing one continuous line.

◀ **Maizie Pfizenmeyer.**
Age 9.

Think about how the student artist used blind contour and regular contour in the drawing.

Creative Expression

How can you develop your ability to observe? Create both a blind contour and a regular contour drawing of a person.

1. Observe the edges and ridges of objects and of people around you.

2. Create a blind contour drawing of the model. Do not lift the chalk from the construction paper as you work.

3. On a new sheet of construction paper, make a slower, regular contour drawing of the model. You may look at your paper, but do not pick up the chalk. The line must be one continuous line.

4. Add several objects to your drawing.

Art Criticism

Describe What objects did you include with the person in your drawing?

Analyze Explain the types of lines you used to create your drawings.

Interpret What similarities and differences do you see between your regular contour and your blind contour drawings?

Decide What strategies did you use to make your drawings successful? Did you improve in your second contour drawing?

▲ **Gu Mei.** (Chinese). *Orchids and Rocks.*
1644. Ming Dynasty.

Detail of handscroll ink on paper. $10\frac{5}{8} \times 67\frac{1}{4}$ inches
(27 × 170.8 cm.). Arthur M. Sackler Gallery,
Smithsonian Institution, Washington, D.C.

Look closely at the ink paintings on these
pages. Mei used flowing lines in her landscape
painting. Hokusai used repeated lines and
concentrated on the contours of the objects in
his portrait. The lines are of various thickness.
Boy with a Flute is a portrait. Both artists
worked directly on paper with ink.

Art History and Culture

Look at the captions and elements in the paintings, such as the
writing in both and the features of the child in *Boy with a Flute*.
What do the artists' works have in common?

▲ **Katsushika Hokusai.** (Japanese).
Boy with a Flute. Edo Period.

Ink on paper. $4\frac{1}{2} \times 6\frac{1}{4}$ inches (11.43 × 15.88 cm.).
Freer Gallery of Art, Smithsonian Institution,
Washington, D.C.

Study both works of art to see how the artists used lines to create flowing contours.

▶ Describe how lines are used in the paintings.

▶ Are the lines all the same? Are some thicker than others?

▶ How do you think the boy in Hokusai's painting is feeling?

Aesthetic Perception

Design Awareness Examine objects with line patterns. How do you use lines to create emphasis in a work of art? What type of brush would you use to make the thinnest lines?

Using Flowing Lines

Flowing lines create a feeling of calm and gracefulness. Flowing lines are fluid; they change direction and size.

You can create **light lines** by adding more water to your watercolor paints, and **dark lines** by using less water. The amount of water you mix with the paint will control the strength of your color.

To create a **thin line,** hold the brush vertically to the paper and touch the paper lightly with the tip of the brush.

To make a **flowing line,** begin with a thin line and gradually press the brush down. Pull up the brush again to make the line become thinner.

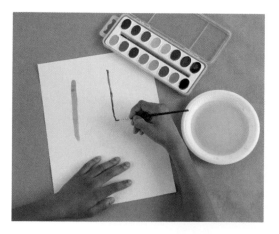

Practice

Create flowing lines. Use watercolors and a pointed brush.

1. Dip your brush in the paint. Use the point of your brush for thin lines and press gently on your brush for thick lines.

2. Practice using different amounts of pressure on your brush to make lines change.

◀ **Shirley Paul.**
Age 9.

Think about how the student artist used flowing lines in the drawing.

Creative Expression

How would you draw a plant using a brush?

1. Examine a piece of bamboo. Notice how it grows.

2. Watch your teacher demonstrate two Chinese brush-painting hand positions. Practice these positions. Then practice the brushstrokes on newsprint using watered-down black ink.

3. Using the same black ink, paint several pieces of bamboo on white paper. Sit straight and hold your breath while making each brushstroke. Remember to breathe before the next stroke.

Art Criticism

Describe Describe the plant in your drawing.

Analyze Did you use flowing lines? Explain.

Interpret Were you successful in drawing your plant? Explain.

Decide If you were to do it over, what would you change?

Shading Techniques

Look at both works of art. Notice the shading techniques used by the two artists. In *Drouet* notice how the area around the face is done with short controlled lines, while the body is created with loose lines. The loose lines create a light value. In his still-life etching, Morandi used closely drawn lines to create a darker value.

◀ **James McNeill Whistler** (American). *Drouet.* 1859.

Etching and drypoint. $8\frac{7}{8} \times 6$ inches (22.54 × 15.24 cm.). Los Angeles County Museum of Art, Los Angeles, California.

Art History and Culture

Notice that both etchings were created during different centuries. Do the time and place during which an artwork is created affect the type of media used to create the artwork?

▲ **Giorgio Morandi.**
(Italian). *Still Life with
Coffee Pot.* 1933.

Etching on paper. $11\frac{1}{6} \times 16\frac{3}{8}$ inches
(29.8 × 39 cm.). The Museum of
Modern Art, New York, New York.

Study both works of art to see how the artists used
lines in shading techniques.

► What types of lines do you see?

► Where are lines close together or far apart?

► Where are the darkest and lightest areas in each
etching?

► How did the artists make certain objects look realistic?

Aesthetic Perception

Seeing Like an Artist Slowly turn your hand and observe how
the light and dark areas change as your hand turns.

Using Shading Techniques

Shading is a technique for creating dark values or darkening an area by repeating marks such as lines or dots. **Value** is the lightness or darkness of a color or object. Hatching, crosshatching, and contour hatching are shading techniques.

Hatching is a pattern of parallel lines.

In **cross-hatching,** the parallel lines overlap each other.

Contour hatching follows the form of an object. If you are creating a shadow on a ball, the hatch lines will curve around the surface of the ball.

Lines or dots placed close together create a dark value. Lines or dots placed far apart create a light value.

Hatching

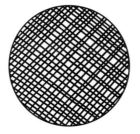
Cross-hatching

Contour hatching

Practice

Use shading techniques to draw a value scale. Use a soft lead pencil and white paper.

1. Divide a sheet of paper into three columns and three rows. Print the name of each shading technique in each box in the first column.

2. Draw lines far apart in the second column to show the lightest value. In the third column, show the darkest value by drawing lines as close as you can without having them touch.

3. Practice hatching in the first row, crosshatching in the second row, and contour hatching in the third row.

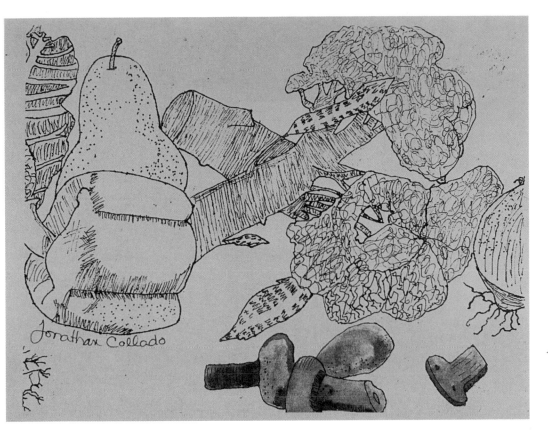

Think about how the student artist used shading techniques in the drawing.

Creative Expression

How can you use shading techniques to show light and dark values? Use shading techniques to show light and dark values in a still-life drawing.

1. Think about ways to portray the value (lightness or darkness) of objects in your classroom.

2. Arrange a still life. Use five or more objects. Set up a lamp or spotlight so the light is coming from one side.

3. Using a pencil, lightly sketch the shapes of the objects. Use a variety of hatching techniques to represent the light and dark areas of your composition.

Art Criticism

Describe Describe the shading techniques you used.

Analyze Do any areas have highlights or shadows? Explain.

Interpret Select a name for your still life.

Decide Were you successful in using shading techniques to create different values? Explain.

Line

▲ **Emily Carr.** (Canadian). *Self-Portrait.* 1939.
....
Oil on wove paper mounted on plywood. $33\frac{5}{8} \times 22\frac{3}{4}$ inches
(85.5 × 57.7 cm.). National Gallery of Canada, Ottawa,
Canada.

Art Criticism | Critical Thinking

Describe **What do you see?**

During this step you will collect information about the subject of the work.

▶ Describe the person you see.

▶ Describe the background.

Analyze **How is this work organized?**

Think about how the artist used the elements and principles of art.

▶ Where do you see vertical, diagonal, and curved lines?

▶ Do you see any lines that look like loose gesture lines?

▶ What kind of view did the artist use for this painting? Explain.

▶ Where do you see contour lines and shading lines?

Interpret **What is the artist trying to say?**

Use the clues you discovered during your analysis to find the message the artist is trying to show.

▶ Does the artist's use of lines make this an active or a calm picture?

▶ Would you like to meet the person in the painting? Why?

Decide **What do you think about the work?**

Use all the information you have gathered to decide whether this is a successful work of art.

▶ Is this painting successful because it is realistic, because it is well-organized, or because it has a strong message? Explain.

Line, continued

Show What You Know

Answer these questions on a separate sheet of paper.

1 Which of the following is not a type of line?
  A. flowing
  B. horizontal
  C. observation

2 A(n) _____ is a quick sketch or action drawing of an object or person.
  A. observation drawing
  B. gesture sketch
  C. diagonal line

3 A(n) _____ drawing is made while looking at an object.
  A. observation
  B. parallel
  C. contour

4 A(n) _____ is the outline or edges of an object or figure.
  A. observation
  B. gesture
  C. contour

5 _____ are used to create light and dark values in a drawing.
  A. Shading techniques
  B. Gesture techniques
  C. Observation techniques

VISIT A MUSEUM
The Wadsworth Atheneum

The Wadsworth Atheneum, in Hartford, Connecticut, is the oldest public art museum in America. It has about 50,000 works of art from the United States and other countries. Bronze pieces from ancient Egypt, Greece, and Rome, and paintings from the past 400 years can be found there. The museum also has the Amistad Collection, which is a history of African American culture. The museum has programs and activities for people of all ages and interests who love art.

▲ **The Wadsworth Atheneum**

Line in Dance and Music

The AMAN International Folk Ensemble performs traditional dances from different ethnic groups who live in America. This photo shows a circle dance from a geographical area of the United States called *Appalachia*. The choreographer uses lines on the dance floor to create a dance.

What to Do Create a circle dance.

1. Form either one large circle or several smaller ones. Hold hands and create a dance. Choose four of these ideas and combine them into a dance using eight counts for each:

   ▶ Walk into the center, decreasing the circle.

   ▶ Walk out from the center, increasing the circle.

   ▶ Walk to the right. Walk to the left.

   ▶ Drop hands and turn in place.

   ▶ Jump in place.

   ▶ Two people drop hands and follow the leader in a snakelike path.

2. Perform your dance to music.

Art Criticism

Describe Describe the four movement ideas you chose.

Analyze What did you do to put the movements together into a dance?

Interpret How did it feel to move in unison with others?

Decide Were you successful in creating a circle dance?

Shape, Pattern, Rhythm, and Movement

▲ **Stuart Davis.** (American).
Composition. 1935.

Oil on canvas. $22\frac{1}{4} \times 30\frac{1}{8}$ inches
(56.515 × 76.51 cm.). Smithsonian
American Art Museum, Washington, D.C.

Shape, pattern, rhythm, and movement add variety and interest to art.

Stuart Davis painted this still life, *Composition*, in 1935. He simplified what he saw and created geometric and free-form shapes. Davis effectively used shape, pattern, rhythm, and movement in this painting.

Artists use **shapes** to represent forms in nature and forms created by people.

▶ What types of shapes do you see most often in the painting?

Artists often repeat shapes, lines, or colors to create a **pattern.**

▶ Where do you see repeated shapes in the painting?

When **rhythm** is used, it creates the illusion of **visual movement.**

▶ Notice how Davis repeated diagonal lines across the work to create visual movement.

In This Unit you will learn and practice techniques to create patterns and the feeling of rhythm and movement in art. You also will review types of shapes. Here are the topics you will study:
▶ Geometric shapes
▶ Free-form shapes
▶ Pattern
▶ Visual rhythm
▶ Rhythm and movement
▶ Flowing rhythm

Stuart Davis
(1894–1964)

Stuart Davis was a painter, printmaker, cartoonist, and graphic designer. Davis was born in Philadelphia in 1894. His mother was a sculptor, and his father was an editor for the *Philadelphia Press.* Davis's paintings often reflect his love of jazz music. His art also displays the influence of cubism, a style in which artists created paintings with split objects, whose various sides were seen at the same time.

Geometric Shapes

◀ **John Biggers.** (American).
Shotguns, Fourth Ward. 1987.

Acrylic and oil on board. $41\frac{1}{4} \times 31$ inches
(104.78 × 78.74 cm.). Hampton
University Museum, Hampton, Virginia.

Look at the art on these pages. *Shotguns, Fourth Ward* represents one of the earliest settlements of an African American community in the city of Houston, Texas. Notice the repeated triangular shapes of the roofs and the repeated rectangular shapes on the railroad tracks. Torres-Garcia's painting is an abstract painting. It contains many geometric shapes.

Art History and Culture

Both artists used paint to tell a story about something that was important to them. After viewing the paintings, name something that was important to each artist.

▲ **Joaquin Torres-Garcia.** (Uruguayan). *Abstract Art in Five Tones and Complementaries.* 1943.

Oil on board mounted on panel. $20\frac{1}{2} \times 26\frac{5}{8}$ inches (52.07 × 67.62 cm.). Albright-Knox Art Gallery, Buffalo, New York.

Study both works of art to find different geometric shapes.

▶ Where are the circles and triangles?

▶ What other geometric shapes do you see?

▶ What things do these shapes represent?

Aesthetic Perception

Design Awareness Look out a window or around your classroom. Notice how the objects are made of shapes. Make a list of three objects, and describe the geometric shapes needed to draw them.

Using Geometric Shapes

Geometric shapes can be described and measured in mathematical terms. They can be drawn with a ruler or compass. The geometric shapes in this lesson are **two-dimensional,** which means they are flat. You can measure the length and width of a rectangle and a square, and the circumference and diameter of a circle.

Here are five geometric shapes:

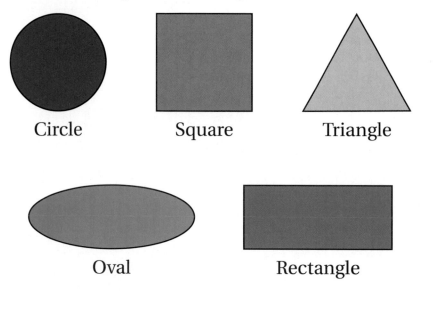

Circle   Square   Triangle

Oval   Rectangle

Practice

Create a drawing of your hand, using only geometric shapes. Use a marker.

1. Notice how each area of your hand can be represented with a geometric shape. For instance, a part of your finger could be drawn as a rectangle.

2. Using geometric shapes, create two drawings of your hand in different positions.

◀ **Chris Gunter.**
Age 9.

Think about three geometric shapes this student artist used in the collage.

Creative Expression

What shapes are the people, places, and things around you? Create a collage based on a theme.

1. Think about a theme for your collage. Make some quick sketches. Use mostly geometric shapes.

2. Draw your best sketch. Add collected materials to make your collage.

3. Before you glue the materials to the paper, arrange your collage until you find a design you like. Use as many geometric shapes as you can. Fill the background with color.

Art Criticism

Describe Describe the subject matter and materials of your collage.

Analyze Where did you use geometric shapes? Why did you choose the colors and shapes you used in your collage?

Interpret Give your work a title.

Decide Do you feel you were successful in using shapes to create objects in your collage? If you were to do it over, what would you change?

▲ **Minnie Evans.** (American).
Design Made at Airlie Gardens. 1967.
. . . .
Oil and mixed media on canvas.
$19\frac{7}{8} \times 23\frac{7}{8}$ inches (50.5 × 60.6 cm.).
Smithsonian American Art Museum,
Washington, D.C.

Look at the art on these pages. Minnie Evans used free-form shapes in her narrative painting to communicate her dreams. Elizabeth Murray's painting is an abstract work that implies the outdoors through colors and shapes. Look for the free-form shapes in these paintings. Also look for geometric shapes.

Art History and Culture

Minnie Evans often used flowers as a theme in her artwork. Can you name other themes that could be shown in several works by an artist?

▲ **Elizabeth Murray.**
(American). *Riverbank.* 1997.
. . . .
Oil on canvas and wood. 112 × 120
inches (284.48 × 304.8 cm.). Albright-
Knox Art Gallery, Buffalo, New York.

Study both paintings to find a variety of shapes.

▶ What types of shapes do you see most often in
each painting?

▶ Describe some of the free-form shapes that you see.

▶ Do these paintings remind you of anything you have
seen or experienced before? If so, what?

Aesthetic Perception

Seeing Like an Artist Think about the various objects in nature
that are made of free-form shapes. Use examples to explain the
differences between free-form and geometric shapes.

Using Free-Form Shapes

Free-form shapes are irregular and uneven. A **free-form shape** is any shape that is not a geometric shape. Free-form shapes are sometimes called organic shapes because they occur in nature. They also can be created from the imagination. These are examples of solid and outlined free-form shapes.

Practice

Use free-form shapes to draw a silhouette. Use a felt-tip marker.

1. A **silhouette** is the shape of a shadow. Many silhouettes are free-form shapes.

2. Look at objects that are made of free-form shapes. Draw a silhouette of one of those objects. Color it solid.

◀ **Brittany Blanton.**
Age 9.

Think about how this student artist used free-form shapes in the painting.

Creative Expression

Have you ever pretended to be in a different world—maybe a city under the sea? Use free-form shapes to create a fantasy painting.

1. Use the computer airbrush tool to create an ocean-like background of blues and greens, with a sand-colored bottom.

2. Use the paintbrush tool to create free-form shapes that look like seaweed and shells.

3. Color the free-form drawings with bright colors, using the paintbrush tool.

4. Save and print a copy of your undersea fantasy painting.

Art Criticism

Describe Describe the objects in your painting. Was it easy to use free-form shapes to create them?

Analyze Did you change geometric shapes to free-form shapes?

Interpret Give your work a title that expresses its mood.

Decide Were you successful in using free-form shapes to represent objects?

Pattern

▲ **Carolyn Mazloomi.**
(American). *Mask
Communion.* 1998.
• •
Quilted cotton and silk. 7 × 7 feet
(2.1 × 2.1 meters). Private collection.

Look at the art on these pages. Mazloomi's artwork is
a symbolic quilt made from cotton and silk. Elisofon's
photograph is a portrait of a man wearing a kente
cloth wrapped in the traditional manner. Can you find
the repeated shapes on the quilt and the kente cloth?

Art History and Culture

Fiber works of art, such as quilts and kente cloths, may include
colors and shapes that represent something important in the
artist's culture.

Study both works of art to find examples of patterns.

▶ Where are lines or shapes repeated in the works of art?

▶ Where do your eyes look first in each artwork, and where do they look last?

▶ How do you think the patterns in the quilt and the kente cloth were created?

◀ **Eliot Elisofon.** (American). *Asante Paramount Chief Nana Akyanfuo Akowuah Dateh II, Akwamuhene of Kumase.* 1970.

Photograph. National Museum of African Art, Smithsonian Institution, Washington, D.C.

Aesthetic Perception

Design Awareness Look at the clothes and other fabrics in your classroom. Find repeated lines, shapes, or colors that form a pattern.

Recognizing Pattern

A **pattern** is a decorative design on the surface of something. Patterns are decorative. The part of a pattern that repeats is called a motif.

A **motif** is something visual that is repeated in a pattern. The motif can be the same each time, or it may vary. In a grocery store, each can on a shelf full of canned goods is a motif, even if the labels vary.

A **random pattern** has motifs that appear in no apparent order, with irregular spaces in between.

A **regular pattern** has identical motifs and equal amounts of space between them.

An **alternating pattern** occurs when the motif is changed in some way or a second motif is introduced.

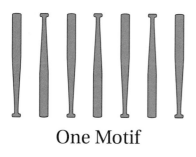

One Motif

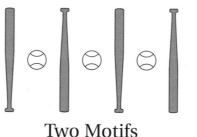

Two Motifs

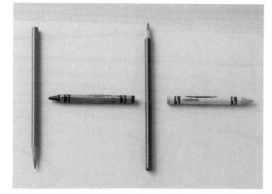

Practice

Arrange classroom objects into patterns.

1. In small groups, collect classroom objects such as pencils, markers, and crayons.

2. Use the classroom objects to illustrate random, regular, and alternating patterns.

◀ **Thomas Garcia.**
Age 9.

Think about what kinds of patterns the student artist used in the artwork.

Creative Expression

Create a paper quilt with a random, regular, or alternating pattern.

1. Cut plastic foam into a shape. With pencil, draw a design on the foam.

2. Choose where you will place the print on the construction paper.

3. Roll a thin layer of ink onto the foam.

4. Lay the foam on the construction paper. Gently rub to transfer the design.

5. Repeat the design as many times as you want.

6. Let the paper dry, then draw and color geometric shapes in the background.

Art Criticism

Describe Describe the motif that you created.

Analyze What kind of pattern did you use?

Interpret Name your paper quilt.

Decide Did you illustrate the pattern correctly?

Visual Rhythm

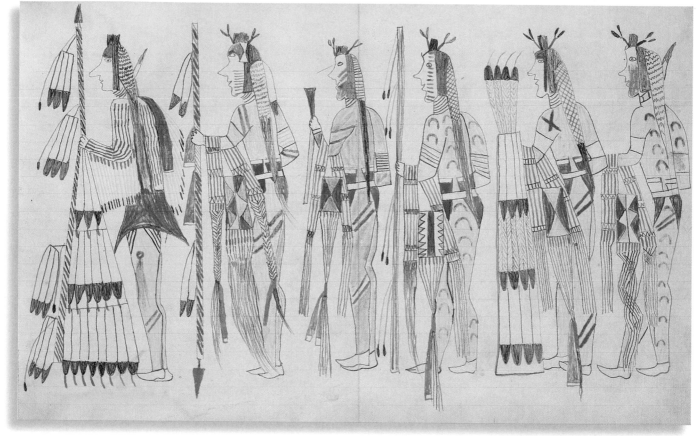

Look at the artwork on these pages. The painting by Chief Black Hawk is a narrative. It was created to illustrate the details of rituals and dress in Lakota culture. Joan Miró's painting is nonobjective. Can you find repeated shapes in these works of art?

▲ **Chief Black Hawk.**
(American). *Crow Men in Ceremonial Dress.* 1880–1881.

Ink and pencil on paper. $10\frac{1}{4} \times 16\frac{1}{2}$ inches (26 × 41.9 cm.). Fenimore Art Museum, Cooperstown, New York.

Art History and Culture

Chief Black Hawk used art to teach others about his culture. What can artists include in their work that would teach others about their culture?

Watercolor and gouache. 18 × 15 inches (45.6 × 38 cm.). Art Institute of Chicago, Chicago, Illinois.

Study both works of art to find examples of rhythm.

▶ Can you identify the beats and the rests in the paintings?

▶ Where is the repetition in the paintings?

▶ Visual rhythms create the feeling of movement as the viewer's eyes follow the visual beats through a work of art. How do these artists create the feeling of movement?

Aesthetic Perception

Seeing Like an Artist List examples of visual rhythm in your environment.

Using Visual Rhythm

Just as in music, a **visual rhythm** has a beat—the positive shape or form—and a rest—the negative space between the beats. In Chief Black Hawk's work, the men are the beats and the spaces between them are the rests. In Miró's artwork the little circles are the beats and the spaces between them are the rests.

The flowers are the beats. The spaces are the rests.

Practice

Create a design that demonstrates visual rhythm.

1. Using construction paper, cut ten free-form shapes.

2. On another piece of construction paper, arrange your shapes to form a design that creates visual rhythm. Remember that the shapes are the beats in your design.

◄ **J. T. Harrison.**
Age 9.

Think about how this student artist created visual rhythm.

Creative Expression

Create a picture of an exciting event by using visual rhythm to demonstrate the visual movement in your work.

1. Think about an activity that has rhythmic movement. The event or activity should involve people, for example, a parade, a sports activity, or a dance performance.

2. Make sketches of people participating in the event. Place the people in uniforms.

3. Plan a composition that will have visual beats (the people) and rests (negative spaces).

4. Draw your figures with chalk on the paper. Finish with oil pastel colors.

Art Criticism

Describe What is the subject of your drawing?

Analyze Describe the beats and rests in your artwork.

Interpret Give your work a title.

Decide Would your artwork have been better if you had illustrated a different activity or event?

Rhythm and Movement

▲ **Patssi Valdez.** (American).
The Magic Room. 1994.

Acrylic on canvas. 96 × 119⅝ inches
(243.8 × 303.8 cm.). Smithsonian
American Art Museum, Washington, D.C.

Look at the art on these pages. *The Magic Room* is a narrative. This painting includes bouncing balls, gymnastic swings, chairs, a window, and a door. *Within the Room* is a nonobjective work about the lines, colors, shapes, and textures in a room. When your eyes follow rhythm in a work of art, you experience visual movement.

Art History and Culture

Artists often use their works to create a mood or a feeling. What is the mood of each painting?

▲ **Richard Pousette-Dart.**
(American). ***Within the Room.*** 1942.

Oil on canvas. 36 × 60 inches
(91.44 × 152.4 cm.). Whitney Museum
of American Art, New York, New York.

Study both paintings to see how rhythm was used to create the feeling of movement.

▶ What types of lines and shapes do you see? What colors do you see?

▶ Explain how the artists created rhythm in the paintings.

▶ When rhythm is used, it creates the feeling of movement, which can be fast or slow. Explain the way the movement feels as you study these paintings.

🔍 Aesthetic Perception

Seeing Like an Artist Look around you. Notice the number of things that look as if they are about to move.

Using Visual Movement

Visual movement occurs when the eye is pulled through a work by a rhythm of beats and rests. Visual rhythm is used to create visual movement.

The beats of the rhythm (used to create the movement) can be shapes, colors, lines, or textures, as well as objects such as people or trees. As in music, visual rhythm can have primary beats and secondary beats.

The beats are the trees, and the negative spaces are the rests.

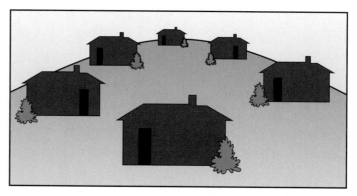

The houses are the major beats. The doors and bushes are secondary beats.

Practice

Use music to illustrate rhythm and movement.

1. Listen to a piece of classical music, such as a piece by Beethoven or Mozart.

2. Listen for the beat. Clap quietly to the beat.

3. Then listen to the melody line and move your arms in the air to represent the movement of the melody.

◀ **Aubrey Silva.**
Age 9.

Think about how the student artist created visual movement.

Creative Expression

Use shapes, colors, and lines to represent rhythm and movement in a piece of music.

1. Listen to music and imagine the shape and placement of the beats. Visualize the line movement to represent the melody.

2. Select related oil pastel colors to represent the beat and the melody. Select dark watercolors to use in the background.

3. Listen again and draw the beats using one color. Press heavily.

4. Listen again, and using a second color, draw the melody lines. Again, press hard.

5. Paint the background using the watercolors that you selected.

Art Criticism

Describe What are some of the lines, shapes, and colors that you used? Are some lines or shapes overlapping?

Analyze What did you repeat to create the feeling of visual movement?

Interpret Do the colors express the mood of the music?

Decide Do you feel your painting successfully illustrates visual movement?

Flowing Rhythm

▲ **Allan Houser.** (American).
Coming of Age. 1977.

Bronze. $12\frac{1}{2} \times 15\frac{1}{2}$ inches
(31.75 × 39.37 cm.). Denver Art
Museum, Denver, Colorado.

Look at the art on these pages. *Coming of Age* was created to celebrate female youth and beauty. Notice the flowing rhythm of the lines in the girl's hair. In Hokusai's painting the smoke creates a flowing rhythm. Also the edge of the snow on the roof of the hut forms a flowing rhythm. This is a landscape painting.

Art History and Culture

Can you think of other works of art with lines that create a flowing rhythm?

▲ **Katsushika Hokusai.** (Japanese). *Winter Loneliness,* from *One Hundred Poems Explained by the Nurse.* 1839.

Woodcut. $10\frac{1}{16} \times 14\frac{1}{2}$ inches (25.5 × 36.8 cm.). Honolulu Academy of Art, Honolulu, Hawaii.

Study both works of art to find flowing rhythms.

▶ What kinds of lines do you see most often in both works of art? Where are the lines located?

▶ Where do you see flowing rhythms in the works of art?

▶ Describe the subject of each artwork.

Aesthetic Perception

Seeing Like an Artist Think of places in nature where you can find flowing rhythms.

Creating Rhythm

One way to create rhythm in a work of art is by repeating curved lines or shapes. This type of rhythm is known as **flowing rhythm.** There are no sudden changes in lines or breaks in the movement. Ocean waves are an example of flowing rhythm.

Curved lines, like the hair in Houser's sculpture, create a flowing rhythm.

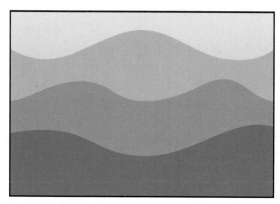

Free-form shapes that are repeated can sometimes create a flowing rhythm.

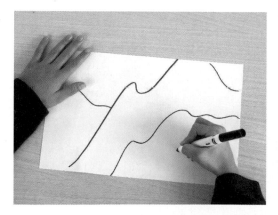

Practice

Create an original design using a flowing rhythm. Use a black marker.

1. Flowing rhythms can be the change of tides, the bark on a tree, or rolling hills. Think about flowing rhythms in nature.

2. Choose an item with a flowing rhythm and create a close-up of a part of that item using repeated lines. Think about how it might look under a microscope and try to reproduce the image.

◄ **Schansa Blackburn.**
Age 9.

Think about how the student artist used flowing lines to create the rhythm.

Creative Expression

How does the wind shape and change lines and forms in nature? Create a flowing-rhythm design.

1. Think about how lines can show rhythm. Cut a variety of curving lines and long, flowing free-form shapes from paper.

2. Arrange the cut shapes on the paper until you get a flowing-rhythm design you like. Then glue down the shapes.

Art Criticism

Describe Name the types of lines and shapes you used.

Analyze What did you repeat to create visual movement?

Interpret What would be a good title to explain your work?

Decide Did you successfully create a flowing rhythm?

Shape, Pattern, Rhythm, and Movement

▲ **John Biggers.** (American)
Starry Crown. 1987.

Acrylic on canvas. 61 × 49 inches (154.9 × 124.5 cm.).
Dallas Museum of Art, Dallas, Texas.

Art Criticism | Critical Thinking

Describe **What do you see?**

During this step you will collect information about the subject of the work.

▶ Describe the people you see.

▶ Describe the setting and the objects in the picture.

Analyze **How is this work organized?**

Think about how the artist has used the elements and principles of art.

▶ Where do you see geometric shapes?

▶ Where do you see free-form shapes?

▶ Where do you see decorative patterns? Where do you see a simple motif? Where is a complex motif?

▶ Where do you see rhythmic repetitions in this work?

Interpret **What is the artist trying to say?**

Use the clues you discovered during your analysis to find the message the artist is trying to show.

▶ Who are these women? What are they doing?

▶ What do you think these women represent?

Decide **What do you think about the work?**

Use all the information you have gathered to decide whether or not this is a successful work of art.

▶ Is this painting successful because it is realistic, because it is well organized, or because it has a strong message? Explain.

Shape, Pattern, Rhythm, and Movement,
continued

Show What You Know

Answer these questions on a separate sheet of paper.

1 _____ shapes are shapes based on mathematical terms.
A. Geometric
B. Free-form
C. Alternating

2 _____ shapes are shapes that occur in nature.
A. Geometric
B. Free-form
C. Alternating

3 A motif is used to create a _____.
A. pattern
B. rhythm
C. movement

4 _____ has beats—the positive shapes or forms—and rests—the negative spaces between the beats.
A. Visual rhythm
B. Pattern
C. Flowing rhythm

5 In _____ rhythm, there are no sudden changes in lines or breaks in movement.
A. movement
B. flowing
C. visual

CAREERS IN ART
Photography

Photographers use cameras to create pictures.

Advertising photographers use pictures to illustrate the layout of an advertisement. They must think about how to make products appealing to viewers.

Photojournalists use pictures to tell stories. They go where news events are occurring.

Fashion photographers use pictures to show the latest fashions. Their work most often appears in magazines and catalogs.

▲ **Photojournalist**

Shape, Rhythm, and Movement in Theatre

Eth-Noh-Tec, an Asian American theatre company, combines music, movement, and words in their performances. They use rhythmic dialogue, body poses, comic facial expressions, and hand gestures to create flowing rhythm. This theatre style comes from ancient Chinese and Japanese traditions. They perform Asian stories with morals about the lives of common people.

What to Do Create a tableau, or frozen picture, of a scene from a class story.

1. Divide into small groups. Your teacher will give you a card that describes one event from a story.

2. Discuss your event and create the event as a tableau. Create visual rhythm with beats and rests in your tableau.

3. Have one person be the director. Other people can be the characters, as well as objects in the setting, such as a tree.

4. Each group presents their tableau in the story sequence.

▲ Eth-Noh-Tec. "Long Haired Girl."

 **Art Criticism**

Describe What kind of visual rhythm did you create in your tableau?

Analyze Explain the decisions you made in order to create the tableau.

Interpret How does your tableau express the main idea of the scene?

Decide How well did you capture the mood of the scene? Explain.

Color and Value

Color is used by artists in paintings, drawings, and sculptures.

A pas de deux is a ballet dance for two. *Pas de Deux is* a combination of acrylic paints, fabric, and canvas. Miriam Shapiro often uses a variety of fabrics in her work to remind us of the traditional household arts created by women.

Artists use **color** to create different moods and patterns.

▶ What colors do you see in *Pas de Deux?*

▶ What type of mood was created in this collage?

▶ Where are the neutral colors? Where are the complementary colors on the woman's head and in the background?

▶ Which shapes do you think are made from fabric?

In This Unit you will learn and practice techniques using color. Here are the topics you will study:
▶ The color wheel
▶ Neutral colors
▶ Complementary colors
▶ Low-intensity colors
▶ Tints and shades
▶ Color moods

Miriam Schapiro

(1923–)

Miriam Schapiro was a leader in the 1970s feminist movement, a movement which led to increased recognition of women artists. In her paintings, she includes fabrics created by women from the past. She calls these works *femmages.* When she travels, she hunts for unique fabrics to include in her works of art. She is also one of the first artists to use the computer as a tool to produce paintings.

The Color Wheel

▲ **David Hockney.** (British).
Large Interior Los Angeles. 1988.
....
Oil and ink on cut and pasted paper on canvas.
28 × 42 inches (71.12 × 106.68 cm.). The
Metropolitan Museum of Art, New York, New York.

Look at the works of art on these pages. Both paintings have a wide range of color. David Hockney used a combination of bright primary colors and neutral colors in his painting. Stuart Davis used a mix of bright colors and unusual shapes. Notice how color is the most important element in both paintings.

Art History and Culture

Use clues such as the furniture design and the gas pump to decide whether the time period reflected in the artwork is modern (done recently) or is from the past.

▲ **Stuart Davis.** (American).
Report from Rockport.
1940.

Oil on canvas. 24 × 30 inches
(60.96 × 76.2 cm.). The Metropolitan
Museum of Art, New York, New York

Study both works of art to find different colors.

▶ What colors did the artists use in their paintings?

▶ How did they separate colors in their paintings?

▶ Do the colors in each piece of art create the same feeling?

▶ If both paintings had been done only in browns, blacks, and whites, would they communicate the same feelings and moods as they do now? Explain your answer.

Aesthetic Perception

Seeing Like an Artist Notice the colors of the spectrum in everyday life. Name things and places where you will find the colors that are on the color wheel.

The Color Spectrum

The colors in the **color spectrum** —red, orange, yellow, green, blue, and violet—appear in the same order in natural light. A rainbow is nature's color spectrum.

Red, yellow, and blue are the **primary colors.** You cannot create them by mixing other colors.

Secondary colors —orange, green, and violet—are created when two primary colors are mixed together. Primary and secondary colors are called **hues.**

Intermediate colors are made by blending a primary color with a secondary color. Red-orange is an example of one of the six intermediate colors.

The **color wheel** is made up of the three primary, three secondary, and six intermediate colors. Notice how the colors are organized so that you can easily understand how to mix a color. Artists use the color wheel to organize colors and to understand how colors work together.

Practice

Create a geometric design.

1. Use a black marker to draw one large geometric shape touching at least two edges of a sheet of paper. Draw a second geometric shape inside your first shape, and then a third shape inside your second shape. Inside each section create geometric patterns.

2. Fill your design with color. In the center shape, use primary colors. In the middle shape, use secondary colors. In the outside shape, use intermediate colors.

◀ **Alexis Lee.**
Age 9.

Think about how the student artist created the color wheel design.

Creative Expression

Using a color wheel, create a background for a scene on a computer.

1. Select the line tool on the tool bar. Draw two diagonal lines that touch the edges of the picture plane. It should look like an *X*.

2. At the center of the *X*, draw a horizontal line straight across until it touches one side of the picture plane. Repeat this on the other side. The white drawing area should now be divided into six areas.

3. Use the fill tool to pour the colors of the color wheel into each area.

4. Use the computer drawing and painting tools to insert objects into the color wheel.

5. Save and print your work.

Art Criticism

Describe Which tools did you use to make the lines and colors in your design? Why?

Analyze Where did you insert the objects? Why?

Interpret What mood does your design express? How do you think the lines and colors help to express that mood?

Decide Were you successful in selecting the six colors? Explain.

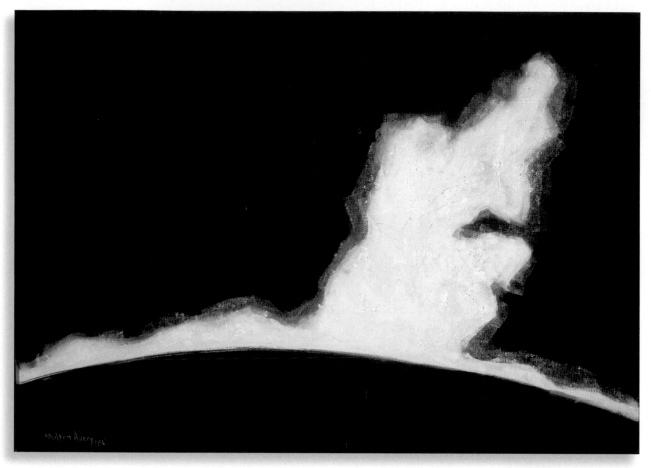

Look at the artwork on these pages. *The White Wave* is an abstract painting that represents an ocean wave. *Rocks and Concrete* is a landscape painting. It was created as part of a series of paintings used to document the building of the Grand Coulee Dam in eastern Washington. Both artists used neutral colors in their paintings. Neutral colors are often used to create a quiet mood in a work of art.

▲ **Milton Avery.** (American). *The White Wave.* 1956.

Oil on canvas. 30 × 42 inches (76.2 × 106.68 cm.). Herbert F. Johnson Museum of Art. Cornell University, Ithaca, New York.

Art History and Culture

Both Avery and Helder painted landscapes. What other artists are known for painting landscapes?

▲ **Z. Vanessa Helder.** (American).
Rocks and Concrete. c. 1940.
••
Watercolor on paper. 19 ×15$\frac{7}{8}$ inches (48.26 × 40.34 cm.).
Cheney Cowles Museum, Spokane, Washington.

Study both works of art to find examples of neutral colors.

► What neutral colors are used in each of these paintings?

► Which neutral color dominates in each painting?

► How does this color affect the overall mood of each painting?

► Describe the types of lines used in each painting.

🔍 Aesthetic Perception

Design Awareness Notice images that were created using only neutral colors. The images could come from books, magazines, or television. What mood or feeling do these images create?

Using Neutral Colors

Black, white, and gray are **neutral colors.** They are often used to lighten or darken a color—to make it less bright—and to create a mood or feeling.

When you **mix a neutral color** with other hues, or colors, you change its **value.** This means that you change the lightness or darkness of the color. Notice how the color below has been changed by adding neutral colors to it.

Practice

Draw a calm landscape using only neutral colors.

1. Create a landscape that looks peaceful and calm. On a sheet of paper, lightly sketch a simple landscape. Focus on simple shapes, and do not worry about including details in your sketch.

2. Use crayons to color your landscape. Make sure that you use only neutral colors.

Think about how the student artist used neutral colors.

🎨 Creative Expression

What colors are used to create a happy mood? What colors seem to set a quiet or sad mood? Select one color to mix with neutral colors to create a mood for an outdoor scene.

1. Create several very simple sketches of a landscape or seascape. Select one of the sketches for your drawing.

2. Use white chalk to transfer your sketch onto a piece of sandpaper.

3. Choose a color of chalk that will blend with neutral colors.

4. Complete your drawings by blending the colors directly onto the sandpaper.

❗ Art Criticism

Describe List the objects you included in your landscape or seascape.

Analyze What neutral colors did you use in your drawing?

Interpret What mood did you create in your drawing?

Decide Do you feel that your drawing is successful? Explain.

Complementary Colors

Look at the artwork on these pages. *Yeihl Nax'in Raven Screen* was made by a family or clan from the Tlingit society. This partition was used to block off a special room at the rear of the house. The most valued clan possessions were kept behind it. The tin canister was used to hold a variety of everyday items. The artists both used complementary colors to decorate these functional works of art.

▲ **Artist unknown.**
(Tlingit, United States).
Yeihl Nax'in Raven Screen.
c. 1830.
· ·
Spruce and paint. $8\frac{13}{16} \times 10\frac{3}{4}$ feet
(2.69×3.28 meters). The Seattle
Art Museum, Seattle, Washington.

Art History and Culture

What are some other examples of utilitarian art?

Study both works of art to identify the complementary colors.

▶ What are the main colors used in each artwork?

▶ How did the artists arrange these colors to create designs?

▶ What similarities and differences in the use of color do you see in these pieces of art?

▶ How do you feel when you look at each of these works of art?

▶ What colors seem to show the greatest contrast in each work of art?

▲ **Artist unknown.** (United States). *Canister.* 1825.

Tin. American Folk Art Museum, New York, New York.

Aesthetic Perception

Design Awareness Look around your classroom. Identify warm and cool colors. Make a list of the warm colors and their complements.

Using Complementary Colors

Colors that are opposite each other on the color wheel are **complementary colors.** For example, red is opposite green, so green is the complement of red. Complementary colors create **contrast,** or differences, in artwork. When complementary colors are used together, they make each other look very bright.

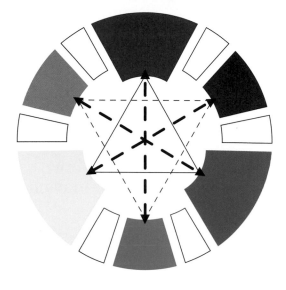

Notice that the complement of each primary color is a secondary color. What is the complement of blue? Of yellow?

Look at the three **sets of complementary colors.** When used together, they can create exciting designs.

Practice

Create a design by experimenting with complementary colors. Use colored markers or crayons.

1. Sketch several simple designs on a sheet of paper. Choose one design and draw it three times on a second sheet of paper.

2. Color each design with one of the three sets of complementary colors. Use the color wheel as a guide.

◄ **Paul Scott.**
Age 9.

Think about how the student artist used complementary colors.

 **Creative Expression**

How would you make a nine-patch design for a quilt? Use complementary colors to make an interesting design.

1. Draw a simple shape inside one of the squares of complementary-colored paper.

2. Cut out the shape carefully in one piece. Cut from one edge, but cut out the center shape in one piece. The square should be in one piece also. Repeat this step four times.

3. Glue the squares to the primary-colored paper. Create an alternating pattern. Then glue the shapes between the squares.

Art Criticism

Describe What is the subject of your quilt design?

Analyze Which complementary colors and shapes did you use?

Interpret How did your complementary colors create contrast and visual excitement?

Decide Would your quilt design be better if you used a different shape?

Low-Intensity Colors

◀ **Artist unknown.** (Melanesia).
Ceremonial Shield. c. 1852.
....
Basketry, nautilus shell inlay on resin base.
$32\frac{5}{8} \times 9\frac{1}{4}$ inches (82.86 × 23.5 cm.). The
Brooklyn Museum, Brooklyn, New York.

Look at the artwork on these pages. *Ceremonial Shield* was woven on the island of Guadalcanal. It was sold to people elsewhere in the Solomon Islands, who decorated it with small pieces of shells. Paul Klee enjoyed the artwork of children because of what he called "the raw energy of the child artist." He often painted and drew like a child in order to capture that raw energy. He was also interested in the masks and costumes that people wore to disguise themselves.

Art History and Culture

List possible reasons why we might not know the name of a person who created a work of art.

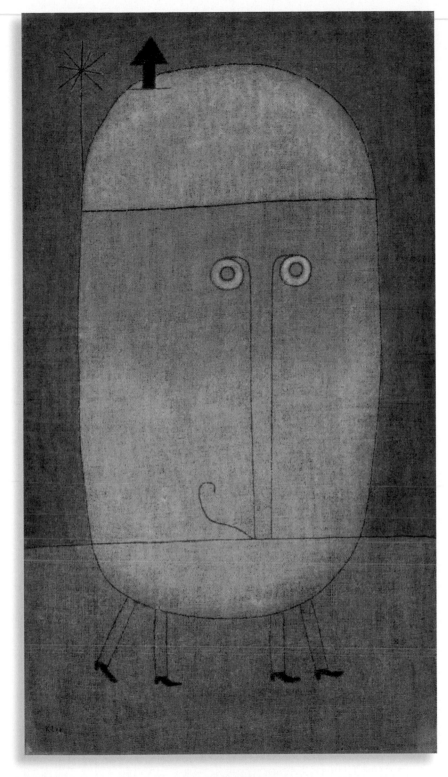

Study both works of art to explain how colors are used.

▶ Name the colors you see in these works of art.

▶ What kind of colors are they?

▶ How does color affect the mood of each work?

◀ **Paul Klee.** (Swiss)
Mask of Fear. 1932.
. . . .
Oil on burlap. 39½ × 22½ inches
(100.3 × 57.2 cm.). Museum of
Modern Art, New York, New York.

Aesthetic Perception

Design Awareness Notice the color of objects you see every day. Name an object that contains a bright shade and another object that contains a dull shade of each primary color (red, yellow, and blue).

Intensity

The brightness or dullness of a color is its **intensity.** For example, because the yellow of a lemon is bright, it has high intensity. The yellow of mustard has a lower intensity because it is a duller yellow.

When you mix a color with its complement, you lower its intensity; it becomes less bright. The more of the complementary color you add, the duller the color becomes. When you add equal amounts of complementary colors, you create a brown or gray color.

Practice

Experiment with intensity by mixing complementary colors. Use crayons.

1. Use one primary color, such as red, and color a light layer on a sheet of paper.

2. Color over the first color with its complement.

3. Do this again, using other sets of complementary colors.

◀ **Cody Ellison.**
Age 9.

Think about what complementary colors this student artist could use if he added animals to his landscape.

Creative Expression

What scenes come to mind when you think of a dull-colored or low-intensity landscape? Use complementary colors to create a low-intensity desert landscape.

1. Use your imagination to identify things you might find in a desert. What colors would they be?

2. Plan a desert landscape by making a few sketches. Include a variety of lines in your sketches.

3. Lightly draw your favorite sketch on a large piece of white paper. Begin by painting your background. Use complementary colors to create low-intensity colors for your desert landscape.

Art Criticism

Describe How did you create low-intensity colors? What problems did you have while painting, and how did you solve them?

Analyze Which set of complementary colors did you choose?

Interpret What mood do the colors in your painting create?

Decide Do you feel your painting is successful?

Tints and Shades

▲ **Wayne Thiebaud.**
(American). *Around the Cake.* 1962.

Oil on canvas. 22⅛ × 28 1/16 inches
(56.19 × 71.27 cm.). Spencer
Museum of Art, University of
Kansas. Lawrence, Kansas.

Look at the artwork on these pages. *Around the Cake* was painted in 1962. *Still Life of Fish and Cat* was painted during the seventeenth century. Thiebaud used light values in his painting. Peeters used dark values in her painting. Both paintings are still lifes. Compare the use of tints and shades in the two paintings.

Art History and Culture

What does the term *still life* mean?

▲ **Clara Peeters.** (Flemish).
Still Life of Fish and Cat.
After 1620.

Oil on panel. $13\frac{1}{2} \times 18\frac{1}{2}$ inches
(34.29 × 46.99 cm.). National
Museum of Women in the Arts,
Washington, D.C.

Study both paintings to see how tints and shades are used.

▶ What are some of the colors used in both paintings?

▶ Which colors are darker or lighter than others? How did the artists create these colors?

▶ What are some similarities and differences in these paintings?

▶ How does the use of color help in creating a mood in each painting?

Aesthetic Perception

Design Awareness Look through images in this book, or think of other images that contain tints and shades. What emotions or moods do tinted and shaded colors create?

Value of a Color

The **value** of a color is the darkness or lightness of that color. Light values are called **tints.** Dark values are called **shades.**

To create a **tint,** mix a color with white. Tints are usually used to show areas where light touches the surface of an object drawn or painted. Tints are also used to show a sunny day and to create a feeling of happiness and joy.

To create a **shade,** add black to a color. Shades are used to show shadows and give the feeling of gloom and mystery to a work of art. Most artists do not use solid black for shadows; they use shades of color instead.

Practice

Create value scales by experimenting with tints and shades. Use tempera paints.

1. Fold a sheet of paper horizontally and open it up. Label the top half "Tints" and the bottom half "Shades." Draw a long rectangle on each half and divide it into five sections.

2. Select a color for your tint. Add a drop or two of the color to white paint, and paint the first section on your paper. Add a drop or two more of color each time you paint another section so that you have a gradual change from a very light tint to the pure color.

3. Use the same color for creating shades. Add black to your color to create shades of that color.

Think about what kind of tints and shades the student artist used.

🎨 Creative Expression

What are some objects in nature that are one color with many different tints and shades? Use tints and shades to create a direct-observation painting.

1. Look at a plant. Notice its basic shape and contours. Lightly sketch the plant. Make sure your drawing touches three edges of your paper.

2. Select a set of complementary colors. Use one color to paint the plant. Add black and white to create tints and shades of that color. Observe the shadows and highlights in the plant.

3. Paint the background with tints and shades of the second color.

🎨 Art Criticism

Describe Describe the shapes and lines in your painting. Describe your complementary-color scheme.

Analyze What did you notice when you were limited to using only two colors plus black and white?

Interpret How do the value changes affect the mood of your painting?

Decide Were you able to successfully produce a painting using tints and shades of one color?

Lesson 6

Color Moods

▲ **Georgia O'Keeffe.** (American).
Blue and Green Music. 1919.
· ·
Oil on canvas. 23 × 19 inches (58.4 × 48.3 cm.).
The Art Institute of Chicago, Chicago, Illinois.

Look at the artwork on these pages. Georgia O'Keeffe created *Blue and Green Music* in 1919. The title of the artwork implies music. Malcah Zeldis painted *Miss Liberty Celebration* in 1987. This painting includes notable historical figures such as Elvis Presley, Albert Einstein, and Marilyn Monroe. Both artists used colors to create moods.

Art History and Culture

Could artwork from a particular region be created using similar media? Note that both paintings were created by American artists.

Study both paintings and notice the similarities and differences in the color schemes.

▶ What types of lines, shapes, and colors do you see? Are any of these elements repeated?

▶ How do you think the artists created the colors they used?

▶ Why do you think the artists chose the colors they used in their paintings?

▶ What feelings or moods are created by the paintings?

▲ **Malcah Zeldis.** (American).
Miss Liberty Celebration. 1987.

Oil on corrugated cardboard. $54\frac{1}{2} \times 36\frac{1}{2}$ inches
(138.43 × 92.71 cm.). Smithsonian American
Art Museum, Washington, D.C.

Aesthetic Perception

Design Awareness Notice the different color schemes you see each day. Give examples of how different color schemes can be used for specific purposes.

Using Color Schemes

Artists use color schemes to create moods. A color scheme is a plan for organizing colors. Different color schemes create different moods.

 **Monochromatic** means "having one color." A monochromatic color scheme uses only one hue, or color, and the values of that color. For example, red, light red, and dark red, if used together without any other colors, would be a **monochromatic color scheme.**

 A **spectral color scheme** uses all the colors of the rainbow: red, orange, yellow, green, blue, and violet.

 A **neutral color scheme** uses black, white, and a variety of grays.

 A **complementary color scheme** uses one set of complementary colors; for example, red and green, blue and orange, and yellow and violet.

 An **analogous color scheme** uses colors that are side by side on the color wheel and have a common hue.

Practice

Create a nonobjective design using monochromatic colors. Use color pencils.

1. Think of a mood. Using one color pencil, along with black and white, create a nonobjective design.

2. Use monochromatic colors to tie the design together.

◄ **Kelsey Mei-Lin Fuller.**
Age 9.

Think about how the feel of this artwork would change if the student artist had used warm colors.

🎨 Creative Expression

What is your favorite color scheme? Select a color scheme to paint an imaginary scene that includes land, vegetation, buildings, and transportation.

1. Think about the way colors affect the look of a scene.

2. Make several sketches of an imaginary scene. Choose your best one.

3. Choose a color scheme that fits your scene. Fill your scene with color.

💬 Art Criticism

Describe Describe the things in your painting.

Analyze What color scheme did you use?

Interpret Was there a particular mood you wanted to create? If so, did you achieve it? Give your painting a poetic name.

Decide Do you feel that using a specific color scheme was helpful for creating a mood in your painting?

Color and Value

▲ **Paul Gauguin.** (French).
Faaturuma (Melancholic). 1891.
....
Oil on canvas. 37 × 26¾ inches (93.98 × 67.95 cm.).
The Nelson Atkins Museum of Art, Kansas City, Missouri.

Art Criticism | Critical Thinking

Describe **What do you see?**

During this step you will collect information about the subject of the work.

▶ What do you see in the closest and farthest parts of the painting?

Analyze **How is this work organized?**

Think about how the artist has used the elements and principles of art.

▶ Which primary, secondary, and intermediate colors do you see in the painting?

▶ Do you see any neutral colors? Where are they?

▶ Which colors have a light or a dark value?

▶ Where do you see low intensity colors?

Interpret **What is the artist trying to say?**

Use the clues you discovered during your analysis to find the message the artist is trying to show.

▶ What is the mood of this painting?

▶ What do you think the woman is thinking about?

▶ Do you have a place you like to go sit and think?

Decide **What do you think about the work?**

Use all the information you have gathered to decide whether this is a successful work of art.

▶ Is the work successful because it is realistic, because it is well organized, or because it has a strong message? Explain.

Show What You Know

Answer these questions on a separate sheet of paper.

❶ Red, orange, yellow, green, blue, and violet are the colors in the _____.
A. primary spectrum
B. color spectrum
C. secondary spectrum

❷ Red, yellow, and blue are _____ colors.
A. primary
B. spectrum
C. secondary

❸ Orange, green, and violet are _____ colors.
A. primary
B. secondary
C. spectrum

❹ _____ colors are made by blending a primary color with a secondary color.
A. Spectrum
B. Hue
C. Intermediate

❺ The _____ is made up of the three primary, three secondary, and six intermediate colors.
A. color wheel
B. spectrum wheel
C. intermediate wheel

VISIT A MUSEUM
The San Francisco Museum of Modern Art

The San Francisco Museum of Modern Art in California was the first museum on the West Coast built to hold only twentieth-century art. The museum has more than 15,000 works of art in its collection. The collection consists of modern and contemporary art, including paintings, sculptures, photographs, architectural drawings, and models. The museum is also known for its wide collection of art by California artists. In addition to the exhibits, the museum offers lectures, special events, and many activities for seniors and children.

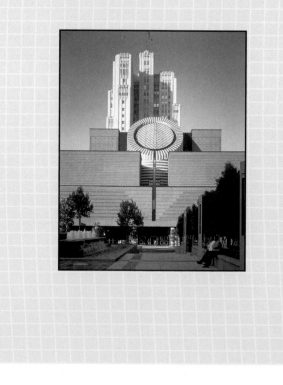

Color and Value in Music

"The Boy Who Wanted to Talk to Whales" is a musical created with very unusual instruments. The color of an instrument is the kind of sound it makes. Flutes and marimbas are different colors in an ensemble. Robert Minden uses ordinary objects such as a carpenter's saw, tin cans, and vacuum cleaner hoses as musical instruments.

What to Do Create a bottle orchestra with a monochromatic color scheme.

Collect empty glass bottles of different sizes and shapes. Experiment by blowing over the mouth of a bottle to hear the sound it makes. The biggest bottle will make the lowest note. Leave this bottle empty; fill others with increasingly more water to raise the sound of the note.

1. Working in groups of six, create the first six notes of a scale (do, re, mi, fa, so, la); each bottle has a different note. Experiment with putting the right amount of water in each bottle to make each note.

2. Sit in a circle in the right sequence of notes. Play the scale from low to high; reverse.

3. With your six notes, play the tune, "Twinkle, Twinkle, Little Star."

4. Pick a conductor to count "one, two, ready, begin" and have all the groups play together.

5. Add two more notes (ti, do) to complete the scale.

▲ The Robert Minden Ensemble. "The Boy Who Wanted to Talk to Whales" excerpts.

 **Art Criticism**

Describe What color do you think of when you hear the sound of blown bottles?

Analyze How did you use water to create the notes of a scale?

Interpret What feelings or moods are created by the sound color of blown bottles?

Decide Were you successful in creating the notes and in playing "Twinkle, Twinkle, Little Star"?

Form, Texture, and Emphasis

◀ **Michelangelo.** (Italian).
Pietà. c. 1500.
. . . .
Marble. 68$\frac{1}{2}$ × 76$\frac{3}{4}$ inches
(174 × 195 cm.). St. Peter's Basilica,
Rome, Italy.

Artists use form, texture, and emphasis to create different types of artwork.

Pietà was created by Michelangelo around 1500. Michelangelo carved many sculptures of people from marble. He created *Pietà* when he was twenty-five years old. To make the adult son look natural on his mother's lap, Michelangelo made her robes very large.

Artists use **form** to create three-dimensional works of art.

▶ From how many sides could you view this sculpture?

Artists create **texture** in their work to show how things look and feel.

▶ How would you describe the texture of the sculpture?

Artists use **emphasis** to control the order in which parts of a work are noticed.

▶ What is the first thing you see when you view this sculpture?

In This Unit you will learn about different ways that artists create forms. You also will learn about texture and emphasis.

Here are the topics you will study:

▶ Forms
▶ Additive sculpture
▶ Subtractive sculpture
▶ Visual texture
▶ Tactile texture
▶ Emphasis

Michelangelo
(1475–1564)

Michelangelo was an Italian painter, sculptor, poet, architect, and engineer. *Pietà* was Michelangelo's major early work. His most famous sculpture, however, is *David*, which was created from 1501 to 1504. The choice of stone for his sculptures was very important because he believed the statue already existed within the marble. Although he loved sculpting, he is probably most famous for his huge painting on the ceiling of the Sistine Chapel in Rome, Italy.

Forms

▲ **Henry Moore.** (English).
Oval with Points. 1968–1970.
....
Bronze. 130 1/16 inches (332 cm.).
The Henry Moore Foundation,
Perry Green, England.

Look at the works of art on these pages. Moore used rounded forms to create his bronze sculpture. His sculpture looks like the figure 8. Lipchitz used black marble to create his sculpture. He used simple, flat forms to create *Reclining Figure with Guitar.* This sculpture represents a person.

Art History and Culture

These sculptures were created in the twentieth century. Do they look like they could have been created in an earlier century? Explain.

▲ **Jacques Lipchitz.**
(Lithuanian). *Reclining Figure with Guitar.*
Black marble. $16\frac{3}{8} \times 27\frac{5}{8} \times 13\frac{1}{2}$ inches
(41.61 × 70.16 × 34.29 cm.).
The Museum of Modern Art, New York,
New York.

Study the two sculptures to see how the artists worked with form.

▶ What kinds of forms do you see in each sculpture?

▶ List the similarities and differences in the look of each work.

▶ Why do you think the artists chose to make their sculptures abstract rather than realistic?

Aesthetic Perception

Design Awareness Look around you. Do you notice the many objects that have three or more surfaces?

Using Forms and Shapes

A shape, such as a square, is two-dimensional. It is flat and can be measured in only two ways: by height and by width.

A **form,** such as a cube, is three-dimensional. It can be measured in three ways: by height, width, and depth. Think of a form as a solid object that has thickness. The following illustrations show how shapes and forms are related.

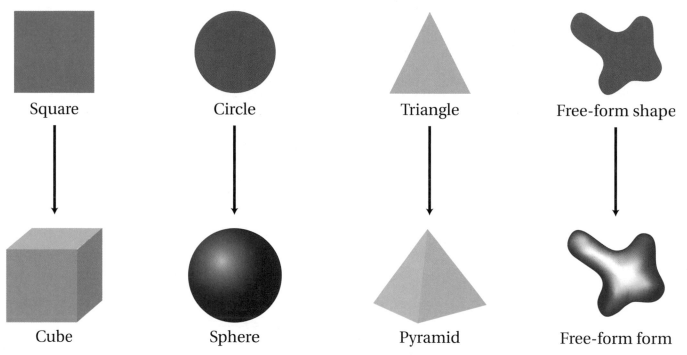

Square   Circle   Triangle   Free-form shape

Cube   Sphere   Pyramid   Free-form form

Practice

Change shapes into forms. Use color pencils.

1. Draw the same shape two times. Color each shape a solid color.

2. Change the second shape into a form, creating the illusion of three dimensions by adding more lines and shading. Blend complementary colors for shadows.

◀ **Aaron Ragans.**
Age 7.

Think about the kinds of forms the student artist used.

 **Creative Expression**

What forms would you choose to create? Use clay to create a three-dimensional sculptured form that is interesting from every point of view.

1. Think about the different forms you see every day. Some are natural organic forms, and some are made by people.

2. Make a large potato form out of clay. Keep turning your form, making sure to work on all surfaces. Use your fingers to press into some surfaces and to pull up other surfaces. Create at least one curved hole that goes completely through the clay.

Art Criticism

Describe Explain how you made your sculpture.

Analyze How did you turn a basic shape into a form? Did you use free-form style or geometric forms?

Interpret Give your work a descriptive title.

Decide Is your form interesting from every point of view?

2 Additive Sculpture

Look at the artwork on these pages. *Standing Ruler* is a Mayan sculpture created between A.D. 600 and A.D. 800. *Woman* by Teodora Blanco was created in 1965. These clay sculptures were created hundreds of years apart. Notice how both forms look more interesting because of decorations.

◀ **Artist unknown.** (Mayan).
Standing Ruler. c. A.D. 600–800.

Ceramic with traces of paint. 9$\frac{1}{2}$ inches high (24.13 cm.).
Kimbell Art Museum, Fort Worth, Texas.

Art History and Culture

Which of these sculptures was created by a member of an ancient civilization?

Study both sculptures to see how the artists used decorative techniques.

► What kinds of forms were used to create each sculpture?

► Describe the forms that were added to each sculpture.

► Which sculpture has the most forms added to it?

◄ **Teodora Blanco.** (Mexican).
Woman. 1965.
....
Earthenware. 27¼ inches tall (69.22 cm.).
Museum of International Folk Art, Museum
of New Mexico, Santa Fe, New Mexico.

Aesthetic Perception

Design Awareness Think about the buildings in your neighborhood. Which buildings have decorative forms added to their surfaces to make them interesting?

Creating Additive Sculpture

Sculpture includes all three-dimensional pieces of art. One type of sculpture, **relief sculpture,** has objects that stick out from a flat surface. Another type, **freestanding sculpture,** is surrounded by space on all sides.

When something is added to either a relief or freestanding sculpture, it becomes an **additive sculpture.** Materials such as paper, cardboard, metal, and wood can be used to create additive sculpture.

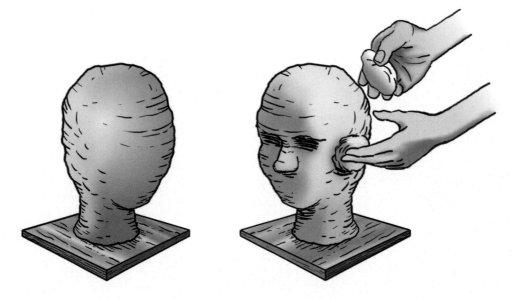

Practice

Build a temporary additive relief sculpture. Use items found in your desk.

1. Create an additive relief sculpture on your desk using only items found in and around your desk. Use a variety of shapes and sizes.

2. Arrange items such as erasers, rulers, and books carefully to make your sculpture interesting.

◄ **Jasmine Krasle.**
Age 9.

Think about how the student artist created the additive sculpture.

Creative Expression

How would you create a portrait of a person using additive sculpture?

1. Brainstorm ideas of people you could portray in your sculpture (soldier, soccer player, football player, police officer, firefighter, doctor, character from a story).

2. Use a cardboard tube or a cone made from poster board as a support. Place a slab of clay around the support. This can be a background support or part of a seated body (even a chair).

3. Create body parts and connect them to the support.

4. Add clothing and tools using thin slabs, coils, and other forms.

Art Criticism

Describe Describe the person you portrayed in your sculpture.

Analyze Is your figure a geometric or free-form form?

Interpret Give your sculpture a title.

Decide What would you do differently the next time you create a sculpture?

Subtractive Sculpture

▲ **Artist unknown.** (Aztec/Mexico).
Jaguar. c. 1440–1521.

Stone. $4\frac{15}{16} \times 5\frac{11}{16} \times 11\frac{1}{16}$ inches (12.5 × 14.5 × 28 cm.).
The Brooklyn Museum, New York, New York.

Look at the artwork on these pages. Both forms are simple and have no additive detail. The Aztec jaguar was carved from stone more than 400 years ago. *Egyptian Cat* was made between 950 and 300 B.C. Notice that although both pieces are carved cat sculptures, they look very different.

Art History and Culture

Do you think cats were important animals in the Egyptian and Aztec cultures? Explain.

Study both works of art to find similarities and differences in the forms.

▶ What kinds of forms did the artists use?

▶ What are some similarities and differences in these sculptures?

▶ Which sculpture has open areas? How does this affect its look?

◀ **Artist unknown.** (Egypt). *Egyptian Cat.* Late Dynasty.

Bronze. $4\frac{3}{4}$ × 3 inches (12 × 7.6 cm.). The Metropolitan Museum of Art, New York, New York.

🔍 Aesthetic Perception

Seeing Like an Artist What is your favorite animal? Think about all the qualities that make that animal unique.

Using Positive and Negative Space

Artists can change a form by carving. When an artist carves pieces away from a form, it is called a **subtractive sculpture.** This is because part of the original material is being taken away, or subtracted.

A figure, shape, or object is the positive space. It takes up room and is usually the first thing we notice when looking at a work of art.

Some forms are created so that we can move around them and see them from all sides. The area around, under, above, and between an object is the negative space. It is the area, or air, around the object.

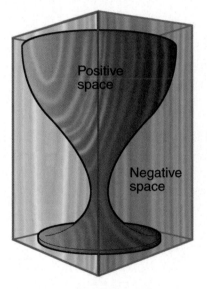

Positive space

Negative space

Practice

Experiment with using positive and negative space in a sculpture design. Use pencil.

1. Draw a square or rectangle. Using the side of the pencil point, color the shape evenly. Do not bear down with the point.

2. Think of a design you would like to create. Using an eraser, carefully subtract the negative spaces and watch your sculpture design appear.

◀ **Nadia Panskey.**
Age 9.

Think about how the student artist created the subtractive sculpture.

Creative Expression

Design a simple animal or free-form sculpture from plaster.

1. Sketch a simple animal form, such as a fish, or a free-form form. Use at least one curve in the design.

2. Tear the cup off the plaster your teacher prepared. Use a pencil to draw your design into the plaster. Draw on all sides.

3. Use a spoon to scrape away the plaster surrounding your design. The design will slowly appear as you carve.

4. Use a paperclip to carve out small areas. Add texture and details. Turn your sculpture as you carve. When you finish carving, lightly sand the areas you want smooth.

Art Criticism

Describe Describe the animal you created.

Analyze What kind of form did you carve? Did you include negative space?

Interpret Give your sculpture a title that includes two expressive adjectives.

Decide Were you successful in creating a three-dimensional form that is interesting from all points of view?

Visual Texture

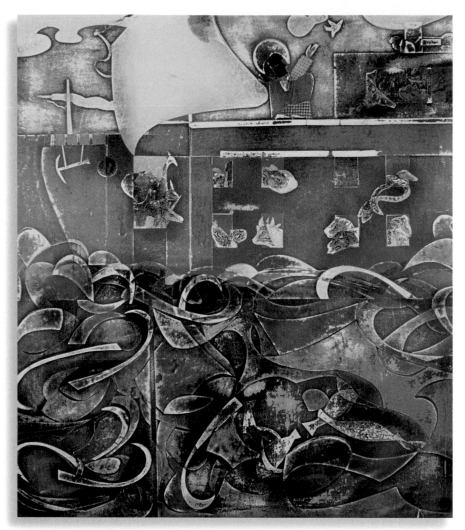

Look at the works of art on these pages. Romare Bearden is best known for his collages made from pieces of old photographs, scraps of paper, and painted paper. During the 1950s Krasner began cutting apart her works and recombining them into collages. Notice the texture of the collages.

▲ **Romare Bearden.** (American).
Noah, Third Day. 1972.

Collage, acrylic on board. $40\frac{1}{2} \times 35\frac{1}{2}$ inches
(102.87 × 90.17 cm.). High Museum of Art,
Atlanta, Georgia.

Art History and Culture

Both collages were created by modern American artists. Can you name any other modern American artists?

Study both works of art for visual texture.

▶ Does the texture of each collage appear to be real, as in a photograph, or created to imitate texture?

▶ Select two categories of texture that fit each collage, for example, rough or smooth, and shiny or matte.

▶ How could the artists have created different textures? If the artwork is rough, how could the artist have made it smooth? If it is smooth, how could the artist have made it rough?

▲ **Lee Krasner.** (American).
Milkweed. 1955.

Oil and collage on canvas. $85\frac{3}{8} \times 57\frac{3}{4}$ inches (216.87 × 146.67 cm.). Albright Knox Art Gallery, Buffalo, New York.

Aesthetic Perception

Design Awareness Use examples to illustrate the difference between real and visual texture.

Using Visual Texture

Visual texture can be created in two ways. **Simulated texture** is texture that imitates the look of real texture. Artwork that incorporates simulated texture looks realistic. **Invented texture** is created when the artist uses lines or other elements to make a textural look without any specific texture in mind.

The four kinds of visual texture are **rough, smooth, shiny,** and **matte.** Textures can be divided into two sets: rough or smooth and shiny or matte. They also can be combined as:

Rough and shiny

Rough and matte

Smooth and shiny

Smooth and matte

Practice

Look for pictures in magazines that illustrate the four kinds of visual texture.

1. Cut pictures from magazines that show visual texture.

2. Divide the pictures into four categories: rough and shiny, rough and matte, smooth and shiny, and smooth and matte.

3. Label each category.

◀ **Caroline Flynn.**
Age 8.

Think about how the student artist created visual texture in the artwork.

Creative Expression

How could you use visual textures from magazines to create a picture that tells a story?

1. Decide on your illustration, and make some sketches.

2. What kinds of things do the textures you collected remind you of? Study them. What can you use them for in your picture? Draw the shapes for your picture on the images and cut them out of the magazine.

3. Arrange the visual texture shapes on your paper and glue them down. Draw the rest of your scene to fill the entire page and color it with color pencils.

Art Criticism

Describe Describe the story you told.

Analyze What kinds of visual texture did you use?

Interpret How do the visual textures that you used affect the look of your work?

Decide Were you able to use visual textures you found to make new shapes successfully?

Tactile Texture

Look at the works of art on these pages. Skoglund used hot-glue guns to attach puffed cheese to mannequins and furniture. She also dressed live models in clothes covered with puffed cheese. Chryssa used steel forms and neon tubing to represent letters in her relief sculpture. The signs in New York City's Times Square inspired her to create sculptures that use letters.

▲ **Sandy Skoglund.**
(American).
The Cocktail Party. 1992.
. . . .
Cibachrome print. 48 × 65 inches
(121.92 × 165.1 cm.).
Private collection.

Art History and Culture

Skoglund's installation includes live models. Chryssa experimented with light. Do you know of any other artists who use unique media?

Study both works of art to find the tactile textures.

▶ Describe the materials used to create both sculptures.

▶ Locate a rough-textured surface in each artwork.

▶ Locate a smooth-textured surface in both works of art.

▲ **Chryssa.** (Greek). *Americanoom.* 1963.

Aluminum, welded steel, stainless steel, and neon. 90 × 108 inches (228.6 × 274.32 cm.). Lowe Art Museum, University of Miami, Coral Gables, Florida.

Aesthetic Perception

Design Awareness Think about decisions you make every day, such as what to eat and what to wear. How does texture affect how you make these decisions?

Using Tactile Texture

Tactile texture is an element of art that refers to how things feel. Texture is perceived by touch and sight. The two basic categories of tactile textures are rough and smooth. Many adjectives describe the different variations of rough and smooth surfaces, such as *velvety, fluffy, slick,* or *bumpy.*

The textures of objects reflect light differently. The way a surface looks depends on how it reflects light.

Rough-textured surfaces reflect light unevenly.

Smooth-textured surfaces reflect light evenly.

Practice

Create a design using tactile texture.

1. Use paper and classroom materials such as pencil sharpener shavings, eraser shavings, and bits of paper to illustrate tactile texture.

2. Create designs on the paper using a pencil, then glue your materials onto the designs.

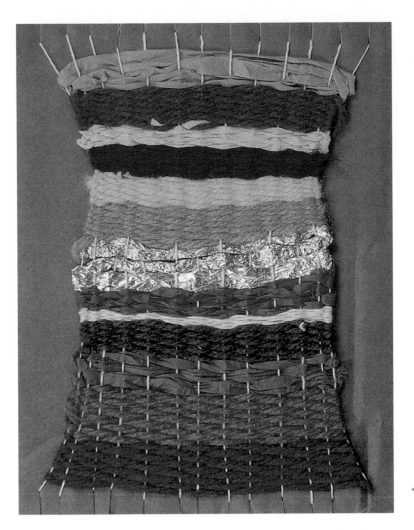

Think about what kind of tactile texture the student artist used.

Creative Expression

What could you use to make a weaving with texture? Use tactile textures to create a weaving.

1. Think about materials you could use for a texture weaving. Collect a variety of materials with a variety of textures, such as yarn, ribbon, leather, and wire.

2. Prepare a piece of cardboard for weaving by notching and stringing the warp threads.

3. Use a variety of textures in your weaving. Think about color variation as you weave.

Art Criticism

Describe List the steps you followed to make your weaving.

Analyze What textures did you use to create your weaving? Are their surfaces smooth, rough, shiny, or dull?

Interpret How can you use your weaving?

Decide Did you include a variety of textures in your weaving?

◀ **Rembrandt van Rijn.** (Dutch). *The Visitation.* 1640.

Oil on oak panel. $22\frac{1}{4} \times 18\frac{7}{8}$ inches (56.52 × 47.96 cm.). The Detroit Institute of Arts, Detroit, Michigan.

Look at the works of art on these pages. Notice the people in the spotlight of Rembrandt's painting. Rembrandt is famous for using light like a spotlight to emphasize the important area, or focal point, of a painting. In *The Meeting of David and Abigail,* Rubens emphasized the two main characters and made them the focal point of the work by placing them near the center and by having the other people in the work look at them.

Art History and Culture

Look at the clothing and the settings of the paintings. Do the pictures represent modern times or the past?

▲ **Peter Paul Rubens.** (Flemish). *The Meeting of David and Abigail.* c. 1625–1628.

Oil on canvas. $70\frac{1}{4}$ × 98 inches (178.44 × 248.92 cm.). The Detroit Institute of Arts, Detroit, Michigan.

Study these works of art to see which areas the artists emphasized.

▶ How did each artist create a focal point in his painting?

▶ Do you see any contrasting colors?

▶ How are the paintings similar and different?

Aesthetic Perception

Design Awareness Think of billboards and commercials. Why are some images bigger or brighter in billboards and commercials?

Using Emphasis

Emphasis is the principle of art that makes one part of an artwork stand out more than any other part. The element or area that is noticed first is the dominant element or area. The dominant area is also called the **focal point.**

When emphasizing an element such as line, shape, form, space, color, value, or texture, make one element more important than others.

When emphasizing an area in a work of art, make that area stand out more than all the other areas in the work.

Practice

Create a drawing of your face.

1. Using a pencil, draw your face.

2. Emphasize an area of the drawing that you want your viewers to focus on.

Think about what the student artist emphasized in this artwork.

Creative Expression

Create a composition that emphasizes an athlete. Choose a sport where the focal point would be on a single athlete in a group of people.

1. Find a picture of an athlete that can be imported into a blank paint or draw file, or scan a picture into a file.

2. Save the picture as a line drawing.

3. Use the paint tool to color in the athlete in bold bright colors.

4. Color in the rest of the picture, including the crowd, in neutral colors.

Art Criticism

Describe Describe the subject matter in your painting.

Analyze What is the focal point of your painting?

Interpret Give your work a title that expresses the mood.

Decide Were you successful in using contrast of value to create a focal point?

Form, Texture, and Emphasis

▲ **Leo Sewell.** (American). *Stegosaurus.* 1984.

Mixed media. 14 × 7 × 20 feet
(4.3 × 2.1 × 6.1 meters).
Location unknown.

? Art Criticism Critical Thinking

Describe What do you see?

During this step you will collect information about the subject of the work.

▶ What does the sculpture seem to be made of? Describe the objects.

▶ If you were to stand next to the stegosaurus's leg, how high could you reach?

Analyze How is this work organized?

Think about how the artist used the elements and principles of art.

▶ Is this sculpture geometric or freeform? Explain.

▶ Is this is an additive sculpture or a subtractive sculpture? How do you know?

▶ Would you say the overall tactile texture of the sculpture is rough, smooth, shiny, or matte? Why?

▶ What is the area of emphasis on this sculpture? Explain your answer.

Interpret What is the artist trying to say?

Use the clues you discovered during your analysis to find the message the artist is trying to show.

▶ Why do you think the artist used found materials for his sculptures?

▶ Do you think this is what a stegosaurus really looked like? Why or why not?

Decide What do you think about the work?

Use all the information you have gathered to decide whether or not this is a successful work of art.

▶ Is the work successful because it is realistic, because it is well organized, or because it has a strong message?

Form, Texture, and Emphasis, continued

Show What You Know

Answer these questions on a separate sheet of paper.

1 In a _____ sculpture, objects stick out from the surface.
A. subtractive
B. relief
C. freestanding

2 A(n) _____ sculpture is created when an artist carves pieces away from a form.
A. additive
B. subtractive
C. relief

3 An artist uses (a) _____ to make one part of an artwork stand out more than other parts.
A. emphasis
B. relief sculpture
C. free-standing sculpture

4 _____ texture refers to how things feel.
A. Invented
B. Visual
C. Tactile

5 Two ways of creating visual texture include using _____ texures.
A. simulated and invented
B. shiny and matte
C. rough and smooth

CAREERS IN ART
Technology

Technology touches all aspects of our lives, including art. Artists use technology to create your favorite games, Web pages, and illustrations.

Computer graphics designers use a computer to create and arrange illustrations, and the layout of a page. They must think about how to arrange shapes and colors on a page.

Digital filmmakers create short films for the Internet. They must think about how to make the film visually appealing to the audience.

Computer-game developers have a variety of roles when creating computer games, including designing the music and sound effects, developing the game, and drawing the characters and scenery.

▲ **Computer graphics designers**

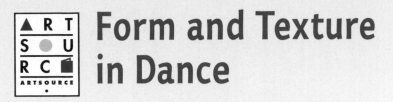

Form and Texture in Dance

"The Nutcracker" is a traditional holiday ballet. A girl named Clara receives a nutcracker for a present. This leads to a dream where she and the Nutcracker Prince visit "The Land of Sweets," where dolls and flowers come to life wearing colorful, beautifully textured costumes.

What to Do Create mime or dances based on toy forms and actions.

In the "Land of Sweets" a variety of dolls come to life and dance. Think about some of the following toys and how you might bring them to life through mime or dance:

jack-in-the-box   ball   spring coils
yo-yo   dolls   computer games

1. Talk about toys with your classmates. Describe their form and think of words that explain how they move.

2. Select one toy that you like. Create a mime or use creative dance to capture the form of the toy, as well its actions. Find variety in the form and movements. Use rhythm. Have a clear beginning, middle, and end.

3. In small groups, perform your "toys" together.

▲ The Joffrey Ballet of Chicago. "The Nutcracker, 'Waltz of the Flowers'" excerpt and "The Story of the Nutcracker."

Art Criticism

Describe Describe the form and actions of the toy you selected.

Analyze What choices did you make in miming or moving your toy? Why?

Interpret What feelings or ideas came to mind as you brought your toy to life?

Decide How well do you think you did in portraying the form and actions of your toy?

Space, Proportion, and Distortion

▲ **John Singleton Copley.**
(American).
Sir William Pepperrell and His Family. 1778.

Oil on canvas. 90 × 108 inches (228.6 × 274.32 cm.). North Carolina Museum of Art, Raleigh, North Carolina.

Artists use accurate proportions to realistically depict people and objects.

Copley painted this realistic portrait of the Pepperrell family in 1778. The Pepperrell family lived in New England until about the time of the American Revolution, when they moved to England. At about the same time, Sir William Pepperrell lost most of his wealth. Notice that Copley used correct proportions to make the painting realistic.

Artists use space in paintings to give the appearance of depth on a flat surface.

▶ How do you think John Singleton Copley created space in *Sir William Pepperrell and His Family?*

▶ Which objects in the painting look closer to you? Which objects look farther away?

Artists use accurate **proportions** to show people or things realistically.

▶ Do you think the people in Copley's painting look like they have been painted with accurate proportions? Explain.

In This Unit you will learn about different ways that artists show size and placement. Here are the topics you will study:
▶ Foreground, middle ground, and background
▶ Perspective techniques
▶ Point of view
▶ Face proportion
▶ Body proportions
▶ Distortion

John Singleton Copley

(1738–1815)

John Singleton Copley was a popular portrait painter during the eighteenth century. When he was seventeen years old he created a portrait of George Washington. In his attempt to capture details and to make his subjects appear natural, Copley sometimes required fifteen or sixteen sittings for a single portrait. Copley moved to England during the American Revolution and did not return to America.

Foreground, Middle Ground, and Background

▲ **Camille Pissarro.**
(French). *The Hermitage at Pontoise.* 1867.
· ·
Oil on canvas. $59\frac{5}{8} \times 79$ inches (151.44 × 200.66 cm.). Solomon R. Guggenheim Museum, New York, New York.

Look at the artwork on these pages. *The Hermitage at Pontoise* is a landscape painting. It shows a village path at the bottom of a collection of houses in Pontoise, France, known as The Hermitage. *Girl in a Boat with Geese* is also a landscape painting. How do you think the artists created the appearance of deep space or distance in the paintings?

Art History and Culture

Pissarro and Morisot were French. What other French artists have you studied?

Study these works of art and notice the placement of the objects.

▶ Which part of each painting appears to be closest to the viewer?

▶ Which part of each painting appears to be farthest from the viewer?

▶ Which part of each painting appears to be in the middle?

▲ **Berthe Morisot.** (French).
Girl in a Boat with Geese. 1889.

Oil on canvas. $25\frac{3}{4} \times 21\frac{1}{2}$ inches (65.405 × 54.61 cm.).
National Gallery of Art, Washington, D.C.

Aesthetic Perception

Seeing Like an Artist Look down at your shoe and then look at the shoe of a classmate who is far away. Which shoe seems to be larger?

Using Perspective

A **picture plane** is the surface of a drawing or painting. There are three terms used to describe the high and low placement of objects on a picture plane: foreground, middle ground, and background.

The **foreground** is the part of the picture plane that appears closest to the viewer. The foreground is usually at the bottom of the picture plane.

The **background** is the part of the picture plane that seems to be farthest from the viewer. It is usually located at the top of the picture plane.

The **middle ground** is the area in a picture between the foreground and background.

Practice

Play a perspective game. Use landscape pictures.

1. Work in small groups. Have a person name an object in one of the landscapes.

2. Another person in the group then says whether the object is in the foreground, middle ground, or background.

3. Have everyone in the group take turns naming objects.

Think about how the student artist created space in this drawing.

Creative Expression

What in your environment could you use to make an interesting perspective drawing? Use perspective techniques.

1. Think about details in your environment that you might include in your drawing.

2. Look through a viewing frame, and do two quick sketches of different areas. Choose one to make into a finished drawing.

3. Divide the picture plane on your paper into foreground, middle ground, and background. Begin by drawing the larger shapes of the foreground. Fill in the middle ground and background. Finish by adding details to the foreground.

Art Criticism

Describe Describe the scene you drew. List the things you included.

Analyze Explain how you used the foreground, background, and middle ground. How did you create the illusion of depth?

Interpret Give your work a creative title.

Decide Do you feel you were successful in creating the illusion of depth? Explain.

▲ **Grant Wood.** (American). *The Birthplace of Herbert Hoover, West Branch, Iowa.* 1931.

Oil on composition board. $29\frac{5}{8} \times 39\frac{3}{4}$ inches (75.24 × 100.97 cm.). The Minneapolis Institute of Arts, Minneapolis, Minnesota.

Look at the artwork on these pages. *The Birthplace of Herbert Hoover, West Branch, Iowa* was painted by Grant Wood in the Midwest region of the United States. *The Bicycle Race* was painted by Antonio Ruíz at about the same time in Mexico. Both artists used perspective techniques to create the illusion of depth in their paintings.

Art History and Culture

Grant Wood was an American regionalist. He painted scenes from his region of the United States.

▲ **Antonio Ruíz.** (Mexican).
The Bicycle Race. 1938.
....
Oil on canvas. 14½ × 16½ inches
(36.83 × 41.91 cm.). Philadelphia
Museum of Art, Philadelphia,
Pennsylvania.

Study both paintings to find examples of perspective techniques.

▶ Find an object that overlaps and covers part of a second object.

▶ Find an object that seems to be close to you. Find an object that seems to be far away.

▶ Find an object with very clear details. Find an object with few details.

▶ Find an object that is painted with bright colors. Find an object that is painted with dull colors.

▶ Find lines that seem to be getting closer together as they move away from you.

Aesthetic Perception

Seeing Like an Artist Look around your classroom. Find objects and lines like the ones you found in the paintings.

Using Perspective

Perspective is the technique used to create the feeling of depth on a flat surface. Depth is the appearance of distance on a flat surface. You saw examples of the following six perspective techniques in the two paintings on the previous pages.

 Overlapping When one object covers part of a second object, the first seems to be closer to the viewer.

 Size Large objects seem to be closer to the viewer than small objects.

 Placement Objects placed near the bottom of a picture seem to be closer to the viewer than objects placed higher on the picture.

 Detail Objects with clear, sharp edges and many details seem to be closer to the viewer. Objects that lack detail and have fuzzy outlines seem to be farther away.

 Lines Parallel lines seem to move toward the same point as they move farther away from the viewer.

Color Brightly colored objects seem closer to the viewer. Objects with pale, dull colors seem to be farther away.

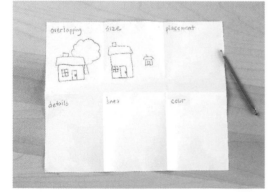

Practice

Illustrate each of the six perspective techniques. Use a pencil.

1. Fold your paper into six equal boxes. Print the name of one perspective technique in each of the six boxes.

2. Draw designs to illustrate each perspective technique.

◀ **Bill Keith.**
Age 9.

Think about the perspective techniques the student artist used in this landscape.

Creative Expression

How can a landscape show perspective? Use perspective techniques in a landscape scene.

1. Think about the things you see in your environment every day.

2. Sketch several scenes you would like to draw. Include all six perspective techniques in your sketches.

3. Select your best sketch. Use chalk to draw the scene, and fill it with color. Remember to use all six perspective techniques to create the feeling of depth.

Art Criticism

Describe Describe the subject matter of your painting.

Analyze How did you use perspective techniques to create the illusion of depth in your painting?

Interpret What kind of mood did you create in your painting? Which element do you think affects this mood most?

Decide If you could redo this painting, what would you do to improve it?

Lesson 3 Point of View

▲ **Michael Naranjo.** (American). *Eagle's Song.* 1992.

Bronze. 12 × 22 × 10½ inches (30.48 × 55.88 × 26.67 cm.). Private collection.

Look at the sculpture on these pages. The images on these two pages show the same artwork from three different views. Michael Naranjo was blinded in the Vietnam War, so his ideas often come from things he saw in his past. The views of *Eagle's Song* from three different angles show his ability to create a three-dimensional piece of art from memory.

Art History and Culture

What other bronze sculptures have you studied?

164　Unit 5 • Lesson 3

▲ **Michael Naranjo.** (American).
Eagle's Song. 1992.
· ·
Bronze. 12 × 22 × 10½ inches
(30.48 × 55.88 × 26.67 cm.). Private
collection.

Study the different views of the sculpture.

▶ What part of the sculpture do you notice first in
each view?

▶ How do the shapes change in the different views?

▶ How do the shadows and highlights change?

Aesthetic Perception

Seeing Like an Artist Slowly turn your hand while holding a
pencil. Look at them from different angles. How does the pencil
change as you turn it? How does your hand change as you turn it?

Using Point of View

A **point of view** is the angle from which the viewer sees an object. The shapes and forms a viewer sees depend on his or her point of view. There are four common points of view: front view, back view, side view, and overhead view.

Notice how your perception changes as you look at the same object from different points of view.

Front View

Side View

Back View

Overhead View

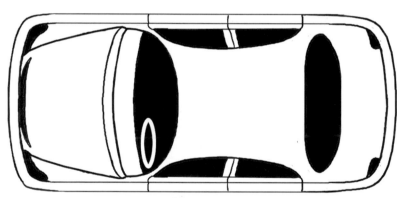

Practice

Describe an object from two different points of view. Use a pencil.

1. Fold a sheet of paper in half. Label each half with the point of view you will be using. Select an object from your desk and study it carefully from two different points of view.

2. Write down the parts of the object you see from each point of view.

◀ **Madeline Jobrack.**
Age 9.

Think about the different points of view of the photographs.

Creative Expression

What object would make an interesting subject to photograph from three different points of view? Photograph a three-dimensional object from three points of view.

1. Think about three-dimensional objects you would like to photograph. Select one.

2. Look carefully at the object you have chosen. Place it in front of you. Walk around it, stand above it, and lie on the ground and look at it. Choose and photograph the object from your three favorite points of view.

Art Criticism

Describe What objects did you select to photograph?

Analyze Describe the shapes in your three photographs and how they changed with each different point of view.

Interpret What point of view is most interesting? Explain.

Decide What could make your photographs more interesting?

Face Proportion Measurements

Look at the artwork on these pages. Renoir and Henri created many portraits. *Portrait of a Young Boy (Andre Berard)* was painted in 1879. *Bernadita* was painted in 1922. Notice the direction in which each subject is facing. Do the portraits appear to be real?

◄ **Auguste Renoir.** (French). *Portrait of a Young Boy (Andre Berard).* 1879.

Pastel on paper. $16\frac{1}{2} \times 11\frac{3}{4}$ inches (41.91 × 29.85 cm.). Norton Museum of Art, West Palm Beach, Florida.

Art History and Culture

Renoir and Henri were contemporaries. What are contemporaries?

◀ **Robert Henri.** (American). *Bernadita.* 1922.

Oil on canvas. 24⅛ × 20⅛ inches (61.27 × 51.11 cm.). San Diego Museum of Art, San Diego, California.

Study the works of art to see how each artist used face proportions.

▶ What is the difference in the position of each face?

▶ Compare the placement of the mouth and the eyes in both paintings.

▶ Where are the ears in relation to the eyes and nose?

Aesthetic Perception

Design Awareness Look at pictures in magazines. Are the faces in proportion?

Using Face Proportions

Proportion is the principle of art related to the size relationships of one part to another, such as a hand to a wrist. Artists use several techniques to draw things in proportion.

Artists use **face proportions** to help place features correctly on a human face. Artists use guidelines, which are lightly drawn lines, which are to more accurately draw both full-face and profile portraits.

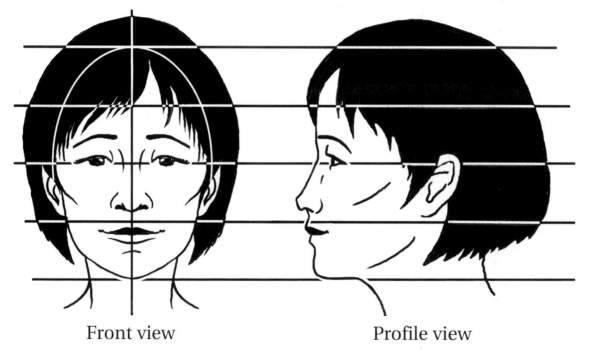

Front view   Profile view

Practice

Practice drawing a profile. Use a pencil.

1. Draw the shape of the head in profile. Add guidelines, using the second drawing shown above as a reference.

2. Add the eye, nose, mouth, chin, ear, hair, and neck.

◀ **Taylor Bontz.**
Age 9.

Think about how the student artist created this self-portrait.

Creative Expression

Spend a few minutes examining your face in a mirror. Draw a self-portrait with accurate face proportions.

1. Draw an egg shape for your head.

2. Draw a guideline from the top of the oval to the bottom. Draw a horizontal line across the center. Divide each half one more time with light guidelines.

3. Sketch your eyes so that the center line goes through the center of each eye. Be sure you have a space between the eyes about the width of one eye. Follow the diagram on page 170. Draw your nose, ears, hair, and neck.

4. Use pastels to add color. Color the background with a contrasting color.

Art Criticism

Describe List the steps you followed to draw your self-portrait.

Analyze Describe the shapes and lines you used to draw the features in your self-portrait.

Interpret What kind of emotion is represented in your self-portrait?

Decide What could you do to the background to make it more interesting?

Body Proportions

Look at the artwork on these pages. Andrea del Verrocchio was an Italian painter and sculptor. *David* is probably his most popular sculpture. Duane Hanson created many life-size sculptures of human figures. His sculptures are so realistic that they are often mistaken for live people.

◀ **Andrea del Verrocchio.** (Italian). *David.* 1473–1475.

Bronze with traces of gold leaf. $49\frac{3}{16}$ inches tall (125 cm.). Museo Nazionale del Bargello, Florence, Italy.

Art History and Culture

Both *David* and *High School Student* are made of bronze. Why do they look different?

Study the body proportions of these sculptures.

► Which artist's work looks more realistic? Explain.

► Can you figure out which objects in *High School Student* were not created by Hanson, but were added?

► How are the sculptures similar and how are they different?

◄ **Duane Hanson.** (American).
High School Student. 1990.
· ·
Mixed media with accessories. Collection of
Mrs. Duane Hanson.

Aesthetic Perception

Design Awareness Think about when you shop for clothes. How
are the clothes arranged?

Using Body Proportions

Although people vary in size and shape, most people have the same proportions.

Artists use the length of the head, from the chin to the top of the skull, to help them in measuring proportion. The average adult is seven and one-half heads tall. A child may be five heads tall, while an infant might be only three heads tall.

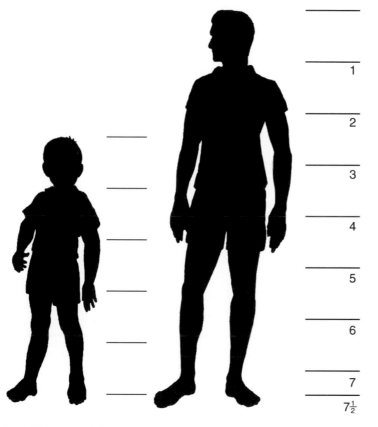

Practice

Compare body proportions.

1. Look through a magazine and cut out pictures of an adult, a child, and an infant. Make sure that the pictures you find are complete images of each person, standing or walking.

2. Measure the head in each photo. Use that measurement to see how many "head" lengths the body is.

◀ **Sarah Bowie.**
Age 9.

Think about how this student artist used body proportion.

Creative Expression

How would you draw a figure with correct body proportions? Use sighting to help you get correct proportions.

1. Study the model and setting. Use sighting to determine how the different parts relate to each other.

2. Place the lines for seven and one-half "heads." Fill the paper from top to bottom.

3. Sketch the figure; use a light color crayon such as yellow.

4. After the sketch is complete, fill your composition with color, texture, and value.

Art Criticism

Describe Describe the pose of the model and the setting.

Analyze What details did you add to your drawing?

Interpret What type of mood does your drawing communicate?

Decide Do you feel you were able to use body proportions successfully in your drawing? Explain.

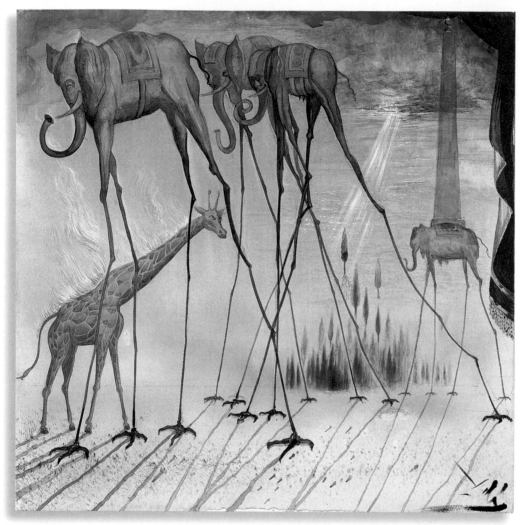

▲ **Salvador Dalí.** (Spanish). *The Elephants* (Design from the Opera la Dona Spagnola il Cavaliere Romana). 1961.

Pencil, watercolor, gouache.
27.5 × 27.5 inches (69.9 × 69.9 cm.).
Indianapolis Museum of Art,
Indianapolis, Indiana.

Look at the artwork on these pages. Both of these paintings include people and animals that do not look normal. The elephants in Dalí's painting have stretched legs and bird-like feet. In Chagall's painting, the cat has a human face, and the man has two faces. Both works of art look like they belong in a dream.

Art History and Culture

Both of these paintings are abstract. What is the difference between abstract and nonobjective art?

▲ **Marc Chagall.** (Russian/French).
Paris Through the Window. 1913.
....
Oil on canvas. $53\frac{1}{2} \times 55\frac{3}{4}$ inches
(135.89 × 141.61 cm.). Solomon R.
Guggenheim Museum, New York, New York.

Study how each artist used distortion.

▶ Which painting has more noticeable distortion?

▶ In each artwork, which images look strange but are not distorted?

▶ What feelings do you experience when you look at these paintings?

Aesthetic Perception

Seeing Like an Artist Think about how a person's face changes when he or she hears good or bad news. What happens to his or her face?

Using Distortion

Artists sometimes use **distortion** to exaggerate an object or feature. Distortion involves stretching, bending, twisting, or changing the sizes of objects from their normal proportions. Distortion is often used to communicate an idea or strong emotion. Enlarged eyes, for example, could suggest fear or wonder. Artists use distortion in paintings, drawings, and sculptures.

Which features have been distorted in the above images?

Practice

Work in groups to act out an emotion using facial expressions.

1. Work in small groups. Your teacher will select the name of an emotion or expression from an envelope for your group to act out.

2. Look at the emotion or expression that was assigned to your group. As a group, practice exaggerating the facial expression assigned.

3. Take turns with the other groups in your class performing expressions. Can you correctly guess the emotions expressed by your classmates?

◀ **Shelby Neesmith.**
Age 9.

Think about how the student artist used distortion in this image.

Creative Expression

Create a distorted self-portrait using the computer.

1. Insert a picture of yourself onto a blank photo-editing file.

2. Convert the picture to a line drawing. Save your work.

3. Choose different areas of your face to stretch and distort. Try moving some features around. Save your work and print a copy.

4. Use a marker to divide the areas of your face into different sections.

5. Color each section using a different color pencil.

Art Criticism

Describe What tools did you use to distort your image?

Analyze Describe the textures and color schemes you used to alter your image. What type of distortion did you use?

Interpret How does distortion affect the mood of your work? Explain.

Decide Do you think you were successful in creating distortion in your artwork? Explain.

Space, Proportion, and Distortion

▲ **Jacob Lawrence.** (American). *Study for the Munich Olympic Games Poster.* 1971.

Gouache on paper. 35½ × 27 inches (90.17 × 68.58 cm.). Seattle Art Museum, Seattle, Washington.

Art Criticism Critical Thinking

Describe **What do you see?**

During this step you will collect information about the subject of the work.

► How many people do you see? What kinds of facial expressions do they have?

► What are the people doing? What are they wearing?

► What is the setting?

Analyze **How is this work organized?**

Think about how the artist used the elements and principles of art.

► Which people or objects look closest to you? Which look farthest away?

► What is in the foreground, the middle ground, and the background?

► Where do you see a part of someone's body that overlaps and covers part of another person or object?

► What is the point of view of this painting?

► Where do you see distortion?

Interpret **What is the artist trying to say?**

Use the clues you discovered during your analysis to find the message the artist is trying to show.

► Which runner do you think will win the race? Why?

► What is the mood of this painting?

► What sounds would you hear if you could go into the painting?

Decide **What do you think about the work?**

Use all the information you have gathered to decide whether this is a successful work of art.

► Is the work successful because it is realistic, because it is well-organized, or because it has a strong message?

Show What You Know

Answer these questions on a separate sheet of paper.

1 _____ is the principle of art concerned with the size relationships of one part to other parts.
A. Proportion
B. Distortion
C. Perspective

2 _____ is the angle from which the viewer sees an object.
A. Placement
B. Overlapping
C. Point of view

3 The _____ is the part of the picture plane that appears closest to the viewer.
A. middle ground
B. background
C. foreground

4 Artists sometimes use _____ to exaggerate an object.
A. proportion
B. distortion
C. point of view

5 _____ is the technique used to create the feeling of depth on a flat surface.
A. Texture
B. Perspective
C. Emphasis

VISIT A MUSEUM
The Smithsonian Institution

The Smithsonian Institution was established in 1846 with money given by English scientist James Smithson. Today there are more than 142 million artifacts and works of art at the Smithsonian. It is also a center for research in the arts, sciences, and history. It consists of fourteen museums, the National Zoo in Washington, D.C., and two museums in New York City. Nine of the museums are located on the National Mall in Washington D.C., between the United States Capitol and the Washington Monument.

▲ **The Smithsonian's first building, known as the castle.**

Space and Proportion in Music

▲ Alfredo Rolando Ortiz *Joropo Azul.*

Alfredo Rolando Ortiz was born in Cuba. When he was eleven years old he moved to Venezuela, where he first heard harp music. He began to learn the harp from his friend Fernando, and then from a master harpist. Ortiz later became a doctor, but eventually gave that up to devote his life to the harp.

What to Do With a partner, make a simple stringed instrument.

Vibration is the basis of sound. Vibration is movement. Sound is the sensation caused in your ear by the movement of air. You can hear vibrations when you stretch a string tightly between two points and pluck the string.

1. Take a small box without a lid and stretch rubber bands around the box. Make sure that rubber bands have different thicknesses.

2. Pluck the "strings" to see if you get different tones, or sounds. The thickness, tension, and length of the strings will change the sound.

3. Decide which lengths or thicknesses of rubber bands produce higher or lower tones or pitches.

Art Criticism

Describe Describe how you made your instrument.

Analyze What did you do to get a higher or lower tone or pitch?

Interpret What did you feel as you created an instrument and heard the sounds it made?

Decide Were you able to get a satisfying musical sound from your simple instrument?

Balance, Harmony, Variety, and Unity

▲ **Judith Leyster.** (Dutch).
The Concert. c. 1661.
....
Oil on canvas. 24 × 34¼ inches
(61 × 87 cm.). National Museum of
Women in the Arts, Washington, D.C.

Artists use balance, variety, harmony, and unity to organize works of art.

Judith Leyster enjoyed painting musical scenes. Based on people in Leyster's other works, the singer has been tentatively identified as the artist herself, the violinist as her husband, and the lute player as a family friend. The figures in the painting have to work together as a unit, "in concert," which has led some people to believe that this scene symbolizes the value of harmony.

Artists use different types of **balance** in all types of artwork.

▶ Pretend there is an imaginary line down the center of the painting. Describe how each half is arranged.

Artists use **variety** to show differences or contrasts in works of art.

▶ Describe the different people you see in the painting.

Artists can stress the similarities of separate but related parts in works of art by using **harmony.**

▶ Which parts of this work look similar?

Unity is the feeling of oneness that artists use in their art.

▶ What about this work makes all the pieces look like they belong?

Judith Leyster
(1609–1660)

Judith Leyster was successful as a portrait and genre specialist. She became one of two female members of the Haarlem painters' guild and had students of her own. She was a wife and a mother as well as an artist. It is believed that Leyster may have managed the family's business and properties.

In This Unit you will learn how artists use balance. You will create personal works of art using a variety of media based on formal, informal, and radial balance. You will learn how artists use variety, harmony, and unity to bring together art elements.

Here are the topics you will study:
▶ Formal balance
▶ Informal balance
▶ Radial balance
▶ Harmony
▶ Variety
▶ Unity

Formal Balance

Look at the works of art on these pages. *Figure from House Post* was carved by a Maori artist of New Zealand. The Maori have many legends to explain their history and the elements of nature. *Model Totem Pole* was carved from argillite, which is a very soft shale. The images on the totem pole, starting from the top, are a bear, two watchmen, a sea bear, a seal, a bearlike figure, and another bear holding a fish.

◀ **Artist unknown.** (Maori/New Zealand). *Figure from House Post.* Nineteenth century.
∙∙
Wood. 43 inches tall (109.2 cm.). The Metropolitan Museum of Art, New York, New York.

Art History and Culture

What kind of tools might the artists have used to create these two works of art?

Study both works of art to find examples of formal balance.

▶ Where do you see repeated lines, shapes, forms, and colors?

▶ What similarities do you see in the two works of art?

▶ If you could draw a line down the center of each work, dividing it in half, how would one half relate to the other?

◀ **Charles Edenshaw.** (Canadian/Haida).
Model Totem Pole. c. 1885.
....
Argillate. 19 × 3 × 2¾ inches tall (48.3 × 7.6 × 7 cm.). Seattle Museum of Art, Seattle, Washington.

Aesthetic Perception

Design Awareness Think about objects you see every day that would look the same on both sides if they were divided in half.

Using Formal Balance

Formal balance is a way of organizing parts of a design so that equal, or very similar, elements are placed on opposite sides of a central line. The central line may be part of the design or an imaginary line.

Symmetry is a type of formal balance in which two halves of an object or work of art are mirror images of each other.

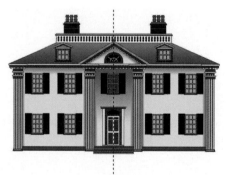

Practice

Look for examples of formal balance.

1. Look through your textbook or books that include works of art and find examples of formal balance.

2. Discuss how each artist used formal balance. Examine each image and see if the artist used exaggeration.

◀ **Dee Scott.**
Age 9.

Think about whether the student artist used formal balance in this sculpture.

Creative Expression

Create a relief sculpture with formal balance that represents you or a member of your family.

1. Curve a foam sheet and make a cylinder form that is twelve inches tall. Glue the cylinder and secure it with paper clips at the top and bottom.

2. Cut geometric or free-form shapes to represent yourself or a member of your family.

3. Add shapes to represent the eyes, nose, mouth, and hair. Use sizes, shapes, and colors to create exaggeration in the face.

4. Attach the face to your post. Use more shapes to create arms, legs, and other patterns on the post.

Art Criticism

Describe Who is the subject of your sculpture?

Analyze What types of shapes and colors did you use?

Interpret What kind of mood does your sculpture create?

Decide Do you like the way your sculpture turned out? Explain.

Informal Balance

▲ **Joshua Johnson.**
(American). *The Westwood Children.* c. 1807.
....
Oil on canvas. 41⅛ × 46 inches
(104.5 × 116.8 cm.). National Gallery
of Art, Washington, D.C.

Look at the two works of art on these pages. Both of these works show the children arranged in informal balance. *The Westwood Children* shows the sons of John and Margaret Lorman Westwood. Westwood was able to commission the portrait from Joshua Johnson at the height of his popularity. Johnson was one of the first African Americans to become a professional artist in the United States. John Sargent created *The Daughters of Edward Darley Boit* for his friend, artist Edward Darley Boit. Each girl is unique, to express her age and personality.

Art History and Culture

Portraits from the past show us what people looked like and how they dressed.

▲ **John Singer Sargent.**
(American). *The Daughters of Edward Darley Boit.* 1882.

Oil on canvas. 87 × 87 inches (221 × 221 cm.). Boston Museum of Fine Arts, Boston, Massachusetts.

Study the way informal balance is used to organize these paintings.

► If you could draw a line down the center of each work of art, what differences would you see in the two halves?

► Which side of each artwork has more people?

► What appears to be closest to the viewer in each artwork?

Aesthetic Perception

Design Awareness Look at your teacher's desk. Do you see formal or informal balance?

Using Informal Balance

Informal balance, or **asymmetry,** can be seen but not measured. Artists use informal balance to organize parts of a design so that objects have equal visual weight.

Visual weight is not measured on a scale. It is measured by which object the viewer's eyes see first. Differences in color, shape, and contour affect visual weight.

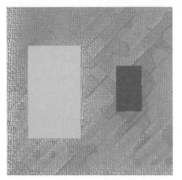

Bright colors have more visual weight than dull colors.

Large shapes have more visual weight than small shapes.

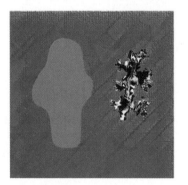

A busy contour, or border, has more visual weight than a smooth contour.

Position, or placement, can be used to create informal balance.

Practice

Use a balance scale to create informal balance.

1. Gather various objects from around the classroom.

2. Create informal balance by adding different combinations of objects on the scale.

Think about how the student artist created informal balance in this portrait.

Creative Expression

Create a family portrait with informal balance.

1. Think of the members of your family. Imagine a time when you are relaxing together. Where are the people sitting?

2. Use a pencil to lightly sketch the scene.

3. With watercolor crayons, fill in the large areas of your drawing.

4. Use water and a watercolor brush to blend the watercolor crayon.

5. After the painting dries, use markers to add hair, eyes, eyebrows, lips, and other details.

Art Criticism

Describe Describe the setting and the people in the portrait.

Analyze How did you organize the portrait to create informal balance?

Interpret What mood does your portrait create?

Decide Would this portrait have the same mood if it had formal balance? Explain.

Lesson 3 Radial Balance

Look at the two works of art on these pages. They are both examples of radial balance. Both pieces were made by folk artists. Folk art is usually made by people who have had little or no formal schooling in art. Folk artists usually make works of art with traditional techniques and content. The styles have been handed down through many generations, and they come from particular regions. Notice how the design in each work of art radiates out from the center in a circular design.

◀ **John Scholl.** (American).
Sunburst. 1907–1916.

Paint on wood with wire on metal. 71 × 38 × 24½ inches (180.3 × 96.5 × 62.2 cm.). American Folk Art Museum, New York, New York.

🏺 Art History and Culture

A painting within a circle is often called a *tondo* in Western tradition and a *mandala* in Eastern tradition.

▲ **William Johnson.** (American).
Lovebird Token. Early nineteenth century.

Watercolor and ink on cut paper. $16\frac{1}{8} \times 16$ inches
(41×40.6 cm.). American Folk Art Museum, New York,
New York.

Study the radial design in each work of art.

▶ Where do the designs begin?

▶ If you turn your textbook, do the designs change? Do they stay the same?

▶ What are the differences in the types of forms and shapes each artist used?

Aesthetic Perception

Seeing Like an Artist What are some objects in nature that are circular in shape, such as a flower?

Using Radial Balance

Radial balance occurs when the elements in a design (line, shape, color, and/or form) radiate, or come out, from one central point. Radial balance is an example of symmetry because both sides of the design are mirror images of each other.

You can find radial balance both in nature and in objects made by people. If you look closely at a flower, you will see that the petals are often arranged around a central point. The top of an umbrella also has radial balance.

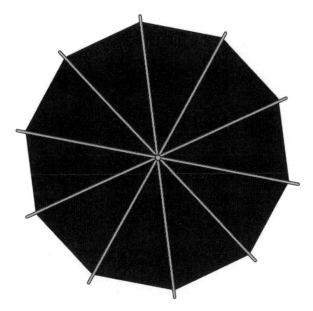

Find examples of radial balance in your classroom.

1. Divide a sheet of paper into two columns.

2. Label the first column *Nature* and the second column *Humanmade*.

3. List examples of radial balance in the correct columns.

◀ **Peter George.**
Age 8.

Think about how the student artist created radial balance.

Creative Expression

Use radial balance to create a wall hanging.

1. Cross wooden craft sticks and glue them together. Glue the end of a piece of yarn behind the center of the sticks.

2. Hold the sticks so they look like an *X*. With the yarn hanging from the bottom, wrap it diagonally over the middle and then over the top right arm of the *X*.

3. Turn the *X* one clockwise turn to wrap each stick. As you wrap the yarn, make sure the rows of yarn lie side by side.

4. Change the color of yarn. Tie the next color to the end of the first piece and continue to wrap. Tie the end of the last piece of yarn and tuck it under. Tie a loop on top as a hanger.

Art Criticism

Describe Describe the design of your wall hanging.

Analyze How did you use radial balance in your design?

Interpret Where could you place your wall hanging?

Decide What changes would you make to improve your design?

Harmony

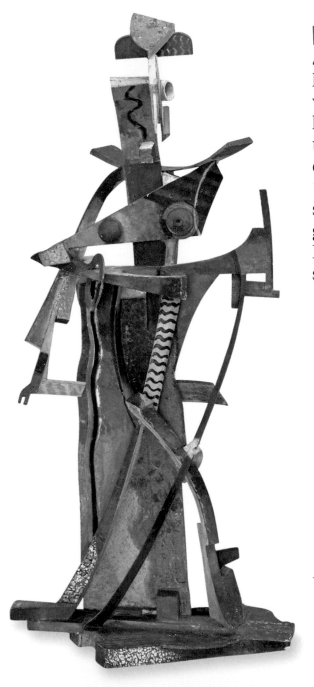

Look at the works of art on these pages. *Symphony Number 1* is made of different kinds of wood shapes and forms and a variety of textures. The repetition of curved lines on the sculpture and on the edges of the shapes and the predominantly warm color scheme give the sculpture harmony. *Three Forms* is a pure white marble sculpture. It consists of only three geometric forms on a block of marble. Hepworth harmonized this sculpture by selecting one color—white.

◀ **Vladimir Baranoff-Rossine.**
(Russian/Ukranian).
Symphony Number 1. 1913.
....
Polychrome wood, cardboard, and crushed eggshells.
$63\frac{1}{4} \times 28\frac{1}{2} \times 25$ inches (160.7 × 72.4 × 63.5 cm.).
Museum of Modern Art, New York, New York.

🏺 Art History and Culture

Baranoff-Rossine and Hepworth created paintings as well as sculpture.

▲ **Barbara Hepworth.** (English).
Three Forms. 1935.

Serravezza marble. $7\frac{7}{8} \times 21 \times 13\frac{1}{2}$ inches
(20 × 53.3 × 34.3 cm.). Tate Gallery,
London, England.

Study both sculptures to see how the artists created harmony.

▶ What shapes and forms are repeated in each sculpture?

▶ What does *Symphony Number 1* look like?

▶ What kinds of textures can you see on each sculpture?

Aesthetic Perception

Design Awareness Look through your textbook for other sculptures. Compare the two sculptures in this lesson with others you find.

Using Harmony

Harmony is the principle of art that creates unity by stressing similarities of separate but related parts. You can create harmony by repeating a shape or color or by using closely related or similar elements.

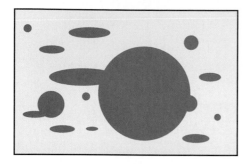

Analogous colors create harmony. They are colors that sit next to each other on the color wheel and share a common color on the color wheel.

An **assemblage** is a three-dimensional work of art made of many pieces put together. An artist can make a harmonious assemblage by using related shapes and colors.

Practice

Build a temporary sculpture on your desk that shows harmony. Use objects from your desk.

1. Create a harmonious sculpture using several objects.

2. Take apart your sculpture and build it another way.

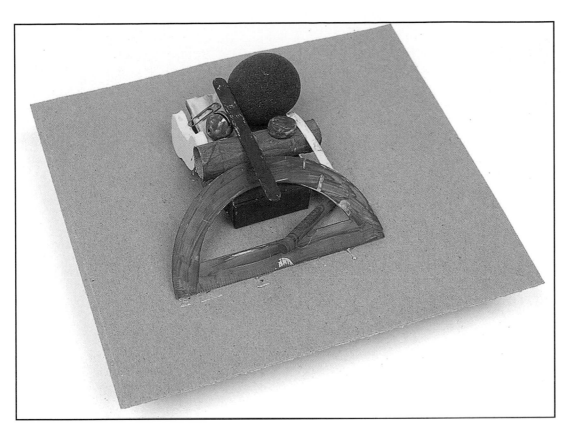

◀ **Cecelia Bonilla.**
Age 9.

Think about how the student artist created harmony.

Creative Expression

What type of sculpture would fit your school setting? Create a model of a sculpture using harmony.

1. Think of the type of sculpture that would fit the environment of your school. Choose an appropriate site for your sculpture.

2. Draw several sketches of how you want your sculpture to look. Select one sketch as your plan.

3. Using cardboard and found objects, build a model of your sculpture. Use analogous colors to create harmony in your design.

Art Criticism

Describe Describe the materials you used to create your model and the site you chose for it.

Analyze How did you create harmony in your sculpture?

Interpret Give your sculpture a title.

Decide Do you think your model is a success? Explain.

Variety and Emphasis

▲ **Georgia O'Keeffe.**
(American). *Yellow Hickory Leaves with Daisy.* 1928.

Oil on canvas. 30 × 40 inches
(76.2 × 101.6 cm.). The Art Institute
of Chicago, Chicago, Illinois.

Look at the two paintings. O'Keeffe introduced variety into her painting of yellow leaves by placing the white daisy at the bottom. The small, busy white petals of the daisy contrast with the large yellow hickory leaves and create an area of emphasis. In Heade's painting, which is full of variety, the focal point is the orchid. The pale lavender color and the silky texture of the orchid's petals make it different from everything else in the work.

Art History and Culture

What do flowers symbolize in different cultures?

▲ **Martin Johnson Heade.** (American).
Cattleya Orchid and Three Brazilian Hummingbirds. 1871.

Oil on wood. 13¾ × 18 inches (34.8 × 45.6 cm.).
National Gallery of Art, Washington, D.C.

Study the works of art to see how the artists created variety.

▶ What do you notice about each artist's use of color?

▶ Describe the focal point in each painting.

▶ What are the similarities and differences of the two works of art?

Aesthetic Perception

Seeing Like an Artist Think of a flower or vegetable garden. What kind of variety is possible there?

Using Variety and Emphasis

Variety is created in art through differences and contrasts. Artists can create variety by adding something different to a design to give a break in the repetition.

Emphasis is a principle of design that makes one part of an artwork stand out more than the other parts. The element that is noticed first is the **dominant element.**

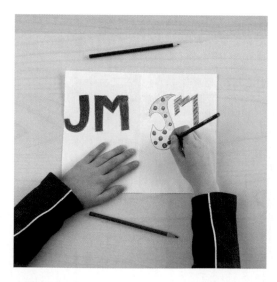

Practice

Use your initials to show variety.

1. Fold a sheet of white paper into two sections. In the first section, draw one design of your initials and color with one color.

2. In the second box, draw an initial design that shows variety. You might draw different patterns or use contrasting colors.

Think about how the student artist used variety and emphasis.

Creative Expression

Create an animal drawing that demonstrates variety and emphasis.

1. Select an animal image or images and develop a sketch. Add a background to the sketch.

2. Transfer the sketch to a large sheet of drawing paper and trace it with a black marker.

3. Color in the animal or animals using crayons to create textures.

4. Using watercolors, paint the entire background in a color that contrasts with the color of the animal, to create variety.

Art Criticism

Describe Describe the animal in your drawing.

Analyze What is the area of emphasis in your drawing? How did you create it?

Interpret Give your drawing a title.

Decide Were you successful in using variety to create an area of emphasis in your drawing? Explain.

Look at the baskets on these pages. Mary Jackson was first taught to make sweetgrass baskets by her mother and grandmother. Along with passing down their techniques through the generations, they also passed down an oral history of their family. The Western Apache basket was used for storage, as a serving dish, for transporting items, and for ceremonial purposes. Both baskets were made using the coil technique. Coiling is a stitching technique in which the coils of the core material are stitched together with a binding material.

▲ **Mary A. Jackson.** (American).
Low Basket with Handle. 1999.

Sweetgrass, pine needles, and palmetto. 16 × 17 inches (40.6 × 43.2 cm.). Smithsonian American Art Museum, Washington, D.C.

Art History and Culture

The oldest known baskets were found in Faiyûm, in Upper Egypt. Tests have shown that they are between 10,000 and 12,000 years old.

Study how the artists created unity in the work of art.

▶ What similarities do you see in the baskets? What differences do you see?

▶ What shapes and forms do you see on the Apache basket?

▶ What colors did each artist use?

▲ **Artist unknown.**
(Western Apache/North America).
Basket. c. 1900.
· ·
Willow, devils claw, wood. 28 inches (71.1 cm.).
Detroit Art Institute, Detroit, Michigan.

Aesthetic Perception

Design Awareness Have you ever seen a basket that is similar to either work of art in this lesson?

Using Unity

Unity is oneness. It brings order to the world. It helps the viewer focus on a work of art as a whole instead of on its individual parts. Unity helps the viewer see what different parts of a design have in common and how they belong together. When an artist uses unity, he or she harmonizes the variety, or different elements or objects, by making them relate to one another.

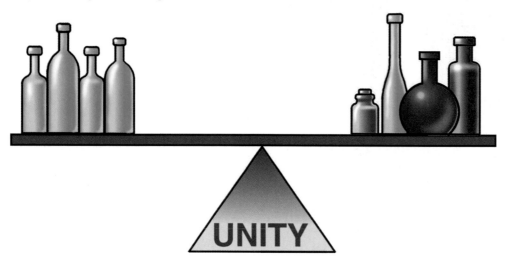

Practice

Look through magazines and find examples of harmony, unity, and variety.

1. On a sheet of white paper, write the headings *Harmony, Unity,* and *Variety.*

2. Find an example of each one in a magazine and glue it under the correct heading.

◀ **Drew Matthews.**
Age 9.

Think about how the student artist used unity in this basket.

Creative Expression

Create unity in a wrapped coil basket.

1. Your teacher will give you a coil that has one end cut at an angle. Refer to page 225 to begin.

2. Continue wrapping the coil with fabric and making stitches on the first row about every five inches apart.

3. To make the sides of your coil basket, place one row of coiling on top of the previous row and stitch tightly. Continue adding rows of coiling.

4. To finish the basket, taper the end of the coil and lay it flat against the last row. Wrap your fabric tightly three times around the coil and cut the remaining fabric.

Art Criticism

Describe Describe the fabric you used in your basket.

Analyze How did you unify your basket?

Interpret If you could enlarge your basket, what size would you make it? What would it be used for?

Decide Were you successful in creating unity in your basket? Explain.

▲ **Viola Frey.** (American). *Family Portrait.* 1995.

Glazed ceramic. 84 × 79 × 29½ inches (213.4 × 200.7 × 74.9 cm.).
Hirshhorn Museum and Sculpture Garden, Washington, D.C.

Art Criticism | Critical Thinking

Describe **What do you see?**

During this step you will collect information about the subject of the work.

▶ What do you see in this sculpture?

▶ What is at the bottom?

Analyze **How is this work organized?**

Think about how the artist used the elements and principles of art.

▶ What kind of balance do you see in this work?

▶ Which form seems to have the most visual weight?

▶ Where do you see harmony?

▶ Where do you see variety?

▶ What is the area of emphasis in this work?

▶ What similarities bring unity to the sculpture?

Interpret **What does the artwork say?**

Combine clues you collected during description and analysis with your personal experiences to find out what this painting is about.

▶ Why do you think the man in the center is so big?

▶ Who are the other people?

Decide **What do you think about the work?**

Use all the information you have gathered to decide why this is a successful work of art.

▶ Is the work successful because it is realistic, because it is well organized, or because it has a strong message?

Balance, Harmony, Variety, and Unity, continued

Show What You Know

Answer these questions on a separate sheet of paper.

1 _____ occurs when the elements in a design come out from a central point.
A. Radial balance
B. Formal balance
C. Informal balance

2 _____ is the principle of art that creates unity by stressing similarities of separate but related parts.
A. Variety
B. Unity
C. Harmony

3 _____ is created in art through differences and contrasts.
A. Unity
B. Harmony
C. Variety

4 _____ helps the focus on a work of art to be on the whole instead of on its individual parts.
A. Variety
B. Harmony
C. Unity

5 _____ is a type of formal balance in which two halves of an object or work of art are mirror images of each other.
A. Symmetry
B. Variety
C. Emphasis

CAREERS IN ART
Illustrators

Illustrators have traditionally drawn pictures on paper to help explain things or make them attractive. Now many illustrators have begun to use computers.

Medical illustrators are professional artists with training in medicine and science who create visual material to help record and distribute medical, biological, and related knowledge.

Technical illustrators collect and prepare information required for the creation of graphics to be used in technical publications.

Marine illustrators are artists with training in biology and science who create visual material to help explain sea animals and their environments.

▲ **Medical illustrator**

Balance, Harmony, Variety, and Unity in Dance

The dance in the picture is based on ranch life in Mexico. The male dancer twirls a lariat that is used to rope cattle. At first he dances alone with the rope, stepping in and out of the twirling circle. Later a female dancer joins him and they dance together in the circle.

What to Do Choose a type of work and create a dance about it, using a prop.

1. List different types of work. What actions are done and what objects are used? Choose an action and a prop to use.

2. Explore the actions involved in the work. For example, practice the action of sweeping with an imaginary broom. Create emphasis by making one part of your action or dance dominant. Use dance elements such as size, direction, and energy to turn ordinary work into dance motion.

3. Share your ideas with a partner. Put four of your best ideas together in a way that creates unity.

4. Perform your dance.

▲ Ballet Folklorico de Mexico. "Danza de Reata" and "Jarabe del Amor Ranchero," excerpts from *Zacatecas*.

 **Art Criticism**

Describe What elements did you and your partner use to give your dance harmony and unity?

Analyze Explain how you used emphasis to change a work movement into a dance movement.

Interpret What moods did you create with your four work movements?

Decide Do you think you succeeded in changing work motions into dance motion?

Technique Tips

Drawing

Pencil

With a pencil, you can add form to your objects with shading. With the side of your pencil lead, press and shade over areas more than once for darker values. You can also use lines or dots for shading. When lines or dots are drawn close together, darker values are created. When dots or lines are drawn farther apart, lighter values are created.

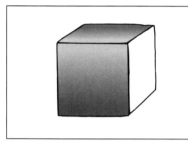

Blending

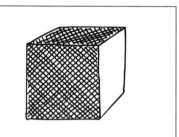

Cross-hatching

Hatching

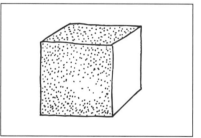

Stippling

Technique Tips

Color Pencil

You can blend colors with color pencils. Color with the lighter color first. Gently color over it with the darker color until you have the effect you want.

With color pencils, you can use the four shading techniques.

Shadows can be created by blending complementary colors.

Technique Tips

Fine-Point Felt-Tip Pen

Fine-point felt-tip pens can be used to make either sketches or finished drawings. They are ideal for contour drawings.

Use the point of a fine-point felt-tip pen to make details.

Fine-point felt-tip pens can be used for hatching, cross-hatching, and stippling.

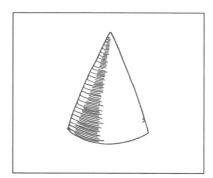
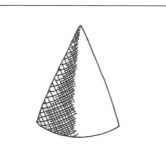
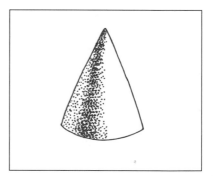

| Hatching | Cross-hatching | Stippling |

Always replace the cap so the fine-point felt-tip pen does not dry out.

Technique Tips

Marker

Markers can be used to make sketches or finished drawings.

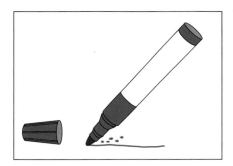

Use the point of the marker to make thin lines and small dots.

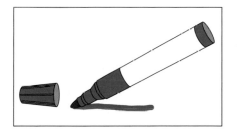

Use the side of the tip for coloring in areas and for making thick lines.

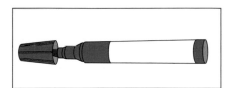

Always replace the cap so the marker does not dry out.

Technique Tips

Color Chalk

Color chalks can be used to make colorful, soft designs.

You can use the tip of the color chalk to create lines and shapes and to fill spaces. As with pencil, you can also use them for blending to create shadows.

Color chalk is soft and can break easily. Broken pieces are still usable. Colors can be mixed or blended by smearing them together with your finger or a tissue.

Oil Pastels

Oil pastels are colors that are mixed with oil and pressed into sticks. When you press down hard with them, your pictures will look painted.

Oil pastels are soft with strong colors. You can use oil pastels to color over other media, such as tempera or crayon. Then you can scratch through this covering to create a design.

Technique Tips

Painting

Tempera

1. Fill water containers halfway. Dip your brush in the water. Wipe your brush on the inside edge of the container. Then blot it on a paper towel to get rid of extra water. Stir the paints. Add a little water if a color is too thick or dry. Remember to clean your brush before using a new color.

2. Always mix colors on the palette. Put some of each color that you want to mix on the palette. Then add the darker color a little at a time to the lighter color. Change your water when it gets too cloudy.

3. To create lighter values, add white. To darken a value, add a tiny amount of black. If you have painted something too thickly, add water and blot it with a clean paper towel.

4. Use a thin pointed brush to paint thin lines and details. For thick lines or large areas, press firmly on the tip or use a wide brush.

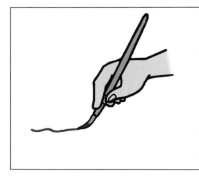
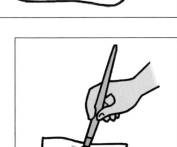

5. Wash your brush when you are finished. Reshape the bristles. Store brushed with bristles up.

Technique Tips

Watercolor

1. Fill water containers halfway. Dip your brush in the water. Wipe your brush on the inside edge of the container. Then blot it on a paper towel to get rid of extra water. With your brush, add a drop of water to each watercolor cake and stir. Remember to clean your brush whenever you change colors.

2. Always mix colors on a palette. Put some of each color that you want to mix on the palette. Then add the darker color a little at a time to the lighter color. Change your water when it gets too dark.

3. To create lighter values, add more water. To darken a value, add a tiny amount of black. If you have painted something too quickly, add water to the paint on the paper and blot it with a clean paper towel.

4. Use a thin pointed brush to paint thin lines and details. For thick lines or large areas, press firmly on the tip or use a wide brush.

5. For a softer look, tape your paper to the table with masking tape. Use a wide brush to add water to the paper, working in rows from top to bottom. This is a wash. Let the water soak in a little. Painting on wet paper will create a soft or fuzzy look. For sharper forms or edges, paint on dry paper, using only a little water on your brush.

6. Wash your brushes when you are finished. Reshape the bristles. Store brushes with the bristles up.

Technique Tips

Chinese Painting

To hold the brush properly, first place the brush horizontally between the thumb and the index and middle fingers. Then move the ring finger behind the brush and in turn move the little finger up to rest against the ring finger.

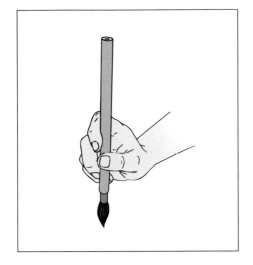 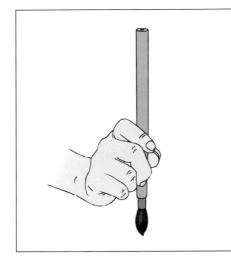

To paint the vertical stroke, rest the wrist lightly on the table. Then lift your elbow about three inches. When moving the brush, move not only the fingers but your whole arm. This allows a wider range of movement and a more accurate motion of the brush.

 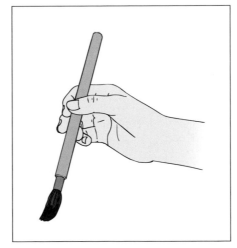

To paint the slanting stroke, place your fingers higher on the handle than you do with the vertical stroke. As you hold the brush, let the handle of the brush slant to one side.

Technique Tips

Printmaking

Making Stamps

Three methods for making stamps are listed below. You can cut either a positive or negative shape into most of these objects. Be sure to talk with your teacher or another adult about what kinds of tools you can safely use.

Cut sponges into shapes.

Using a pencil, clay tool, tip of a paper clip, or another object, draw or sculpt a design on a flat piece of modeling clay.

Using a pencil, tip of a paper clip, or another object, draw or sculpt a design on a flat piece of plastic foam.

Technique Tips

Printing Stamps

1. Put a small amount of water-based printing ink or some paint onto a hard, flat surface. Roll a softer roller, called a brayer, back and forth in the ink until there is an even coating of paint on both the surface and the brayer.

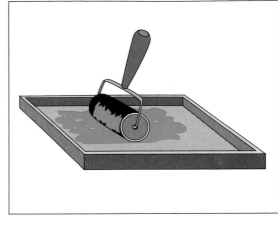

2. Roll the brayer filled with ink over the printing stamp. The ink should cover the stamp evenly without going into the grooves of your design.

3. You can also use a brush to coat the stamp evenly with paint. Whichever method you use, be careful not to use too much ink or paint.

4. Gently press your stamp onto your paper. Then peel the paper and stamp apart and check your print. If you wish to make several prints of your design, you should ink your stamp again as needed.

5. When you have finished, wash the brayer, the surface, and the stamp.

Technique Tips

Collage

In a collage, objects or pieces of paper, fabric, or other materials are pasted onto a surface to create a work of art. When planning your collage, consider such things as:

- Size of shapes and spaces
- Placement of shapes and spaces
- Color schemes
- Textures

Remember that the empty (negative) spaces are also part of your design. Plan a collage as you would plan a painting or a drawing. After deciding what shapes and objects you want to use, arrange them on the paper. When you have made an arrangement you like, glue your shapes and objects to the paper.

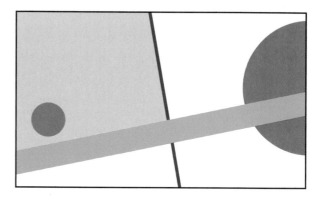

Weaving

1. Measure and cut notches one-quarter inch apart and one-half inch deep on opposite sides of the cardboard.
2. Tape the warp thread to the back and string from top to bottom. Continue to wrap the thread through each notch until you reach the end. Tape the end of the thread to the cardboard.
3. Start to weave horizontally at the bottom of the loom in an over-one-under-one motion.
4. Do not pull the weft threads too tight.

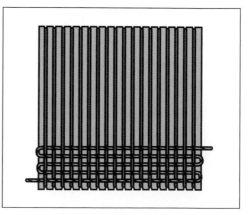

Technique Tips

Coiled Basket

1. Bend the tapered end against itself and begin wrapping with your first strip of fabric.

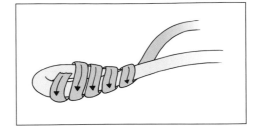

2. Once the tapered end is secure, begin wrapping a single coil until about five inches of coil is covered.

3. Secure the first row by wrapping a stitch into the center opening.

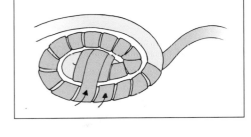

4. Continue wrapping the coil with fabric. About every five inches, attach a stitch onto the last row. The holding stitch goes over one row only.

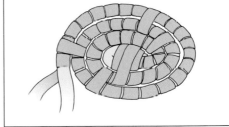

5. To make the side of the coil basket, place one row of coiling on top of the previous row and stitch tightly.

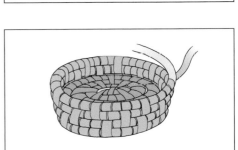

6. To finish the basket, taper the end and lay it flat against the last row. Wrap your fabric tightly three times and cut the remaining fabric.

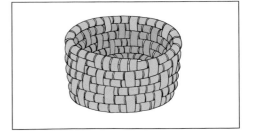

Technique Tips

Sculpting

Clay

Pinch and pull clay into the desired shape.

Joining two pieces of clay

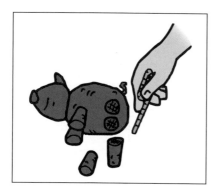

Score, or scratch, both pieces so they will stick together.

Attach the pieces with some *slip,* which is watery clay.

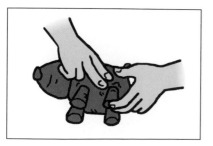

Squeeze the two pieces together. *Smooth* the edges.

Technique Tips

Clay Slab Construction

To roll a slab of clay, press a ball of clay into a flat shape on a cloth-covered board. Place one one-quarter-inch slat on each side of the clay. Use a roller to press the slab into an even thickness. With a straightened paper clip, trim the slab into the desired shape.

Wrap unfinished sculptures in plastic to keep them moist until finished.

When you are constructing a form such as a container or a house with slabs of clay, it may be necessary to stuff the form with wads of newspaper to support the walls. The newspaper will burn out in the kiln.

Soap and Plaster Sculpture

You can carve sculptures from clay, soap, or plaster forms. Draw the basic shape of your idea onto all sides of the form. Keep your design simple. Carve a little bit at a time, using a spoon, a paper clip, or a plastic knife, while constantly turning your form.

Activity Tips

Unit 1 · Lesson 1 **Types of Lines**

🎨 Creative Expression

1. Think about a cause that concerns you, such as pollution. Write a short slogan or message that expresses your concerns.

2. Design a poster about your cause. Use the different kinds of lines and line variations that you saw in the artwork. Plan a way to work your slogan into a design, like Jaune Quick-to-See Smith did.

Unit 1 · Lesson 2 **Gesture Drawings**

🎨 Creative Expression

1. Think about how action is captured in a drawing. Use quick, sketchy lines.

2. Take turns with classmates freezing in a movement. Hold poses for 30 seconds. Each time you draw someone new, change the crayon color.

3. Repeat lines and shapes and let your figures overlap to fill the entire page.

Activity Tips

Unit 1 · Lesson 3 **Observation Drawings**

 **Creative Expression**

1. Think about repeating lines and shapes to draw gestures.

2. Go to the school playground and watch all the action that is taking place.

3. Sketch a variety of gestures from a specific point of view. Show the gestures from a specific point of view. Show the gestures of the children and some of their environment. Fill the entire page. Be sure to overlap your objects and use a variety of lines.

Unit 1 · Lesson 4 **Contour Lines**

Creative Expression

1. Observe the edges and ridges of objects and of people around you.

2. Create a blind contour drawing of the model. Do not lift the chalk from the construction paper as you work.

3. On a new sheet of construction paper, make a slower, regular contour drawing of the model. You may look at your paper, but do not pick up the chalk. The line must be one continuous line.

4. Add several objects to your drawing.

Activity Tips

Flowing Lines

🎨 Creative Expression

1. Examine a piece of bamboo. Notice how it grows.

2. Watch your teacher demonstrate two Chinese brush-painting hand positions. Practice these positions. Then practice the brushstrokes on newsprint using watered-down black ink.

3. Using the same black ink, paint several pieces of bamboo on white paper. Sit straight and hold your breath while making each brushstroke. Remember to breathe before the next stroke.

Shading Techniques

🎨 Creative Expression

1. Think about ways to portray the value (lightness or darkness) of objects in your classroom.

2. Arrange a still life. Use five or more objects. Set up a lamp or spotlight so the light is coming from one side.

3. Using a pencil, lightly sketch the shapes of the objects. Use a variety of hatching techniques to represent the light and dark areas of your composition.

Activity Tips

Unit 2 · Lesson 1 Geometric Shapes

Creative Expression

1. Think about a theme for your collage. Make some quick sketches. Use mostly geometric shapes.

2. Draw your best sketch. Add collected materials to make your collage.

3. Before you glue the materials to the paper, arrange your collage until you find a design you like. Use as many geometric shapes as you can. Fill the background with color.

Unit 2 · Lesson 2 Free-Form Shapes

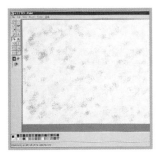

Creative Expression

1. Use the computer airbrush tool to create an ocean-like background of blues and greens, with a sand-colored bottom.

2. Use the paintbrush tool to create free-form shapes that look like seaweed and shells.

3. Color the free-form drawings with bright colors, using the paintbrush tool.

4. Save and print a copy of your undersea fantasy painting.

Activity Tips

Pattern

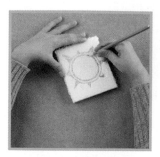

🎨 Creative Expression

1. Cut plastic foam into a shape. With pencil, draw a design on the foam.

2. Choose where you will place the print on the construction paper.

3. Roll a thin layer of ink onto the foam.

4. Lay the foam on the construction paper. Gently rub to transfer the design.

5. Repeat the design as many times as you want.

6. Let the paper dry, then draw and color geometric shapes in the background.

Visual Rhythm

🎨 Creative Expression

1. Think about an activity that has rhythmic movement. The event or activity should involve people, for example, a parade, a sports activity, or a dance performance.

2. Make sketches of people participating in the event. Place the people in uniforms.

3. Plan a composition that will have visual beats (the people) and rests (negative spaces).

4. Draw your figures with chalk on the paper. Finish with oil pastel colors.

Activity Tips

Rhythm and Movement

Creative Expression

1. Listen to music and imagine the shape and placement of the beats. Visualize the line movement to represent the melody.

2. Select related oil pastel colors to represent the beat and the melody. Select dark watercolors to use in the background.

3. Listen again and draw the beats using one color. Press heavily.

4. Listen again, and using a second color, draw the melody lines. Again, press hard.

5. Paint the background using the watercolors that you selected.

Flowing Rhythm

Creative Expression

1. Think about how lines can show rhythm. Cut a variety of curving lines and long, flowing free-form shapes from paper.

2. Arrange the cut shapes on the paper until you get a flowing-rhythm design you like. Then glue down the shapes.

Activity Tips

The Color Wheel

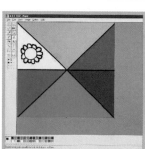

🎨 Creative Expression

1. Select the line tool on the tool bar. Draw two diagonal lines that touch the edges of the picture plane. It should look like an *X*.

2. At the center of the *X*, draw a horizontal line straight across until it touches one side of the picture plane. Repeat this on the other side. The white drawing area should now be divided into six areas.

3. Use the fill tool to pour the colors of the color wheel into each area.

4. Use the drawing and painting tools to insert objects into the color wheel. Save and print the file.

Neutral Colors

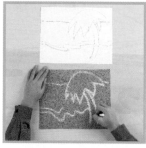

🎨 Creative Expression

1. Create several very simple sketches of a landscape or seascape. Select one of the sketches for your drawing.

2. Use white chalk to transfer your sketch onto a piece of sandpaper.

3. Choose a color of chalk that will blend with neutral colors.

4. Complete your drawings by blending the colors directly onto the sandpaper.

Activity Tips

Complementary Colors

Creative Expression

1. Draw a simple shape inside one of the squares of complementary-colored paper.

2. Cut out the shape carefully in one piece. Cut from one edge, but cut out the center shape in one piece. The square should be in one piece also. Repeat this step four times.

3. Glue the squares to the primary-colored paper. Create an alternating pattern. Then glue the shapes between the squares.

Low-Intensity Colors

Creative Expression

1. Use your imagination to identify things you might find in a desert. What colors would they be?

2. Plan a desert landscape by making a few sketches. Include a variety of lines in your sketches.

3. Lightly draw your favorite sketch on a large piece of white paper. Begin by painting your background. Use complementary colors to create low-intensity colors for your desert landscape.

Activity Tips

Tints and Shades

🎨 Creative Expression

1. Look at a plant. Notice its basic shape and contours. Lightly sketch the plant. Make sure your drawing touches three edges of your paper.

2. Select a set of complementary colors. Use one color to paint the plant. Add black and white to create tints and shades of that color. Observe the shadows and highlights in the plant.

3. Paint the background with tints and shades of the second color.

Color Moods

🎨 Creative Expression

1. Think about the way colors affect the look of a scene.

2. Make several sketches of an imaginary scene. Choose your best one.

3. Choose a color scheme that fits your scene. Fill your scene with color.

Activity Tips

Forms

🎨 Creative Expression

1. Think about the different forms you see every day. Some are natural organic forms, and some are made by people.

2. Make a large potato form out of clay. Keep turning your form, making sure to work on all surfaces. Use your fingers to press into some surfaces and to pull up other surfaces. Create at least one curved hole that goes completely through the clay.

....

Unit 4 · Lesson 2 **Additive Sculpture**

🎨 Creative Expression

1. Brainstorm ideas of people you could portray in your sculpture (soldier, soccer player, football player, police officer, firefighter, doctor, character from a story).

2. Use a cardboard tube or a cone made from poster board as a support. Place a slab of clay around the support. This can be a background support or part of a seated body (even a chair).

3. Create body parts and connect them to the support.

4. Add clothing and tools using thin slabs, coils, and other forms.

Activity Tips

Subtractive Sculpture

 Creative Expression

1. Sketch a simple animal form, such as a fish, or a free-form form. Use at least one curve in the design.

2. Tear the cup off the plaster your teacher prepared. Use a pencil to draw your design into the plaster. Draw on all sides.

3. Use a spoon to scrape away the plaster surrounding your design. The design will slowly appear as you carve.

4. Use a paperclip to carve out small areas. Add texture and detail. Turn your sculpture as you carve. When you finish carving, lightly sand the areas you want smooth.

Visual Texture

Creative Expression

1. Decide on your illustration, and make some sketches.

2. What kinds of things do the textures you collected remind you of? Study them. What can you use them for in your picture? Draw the shapes for your picture on the images and cut them out of the magazine.

3. Arrange the visual texture shapes on your paper and glue them down. Draw the rest of your scene to fill the entire page and color it with color pencils.

Activity Tips

Tactile Texture

Creative Expression

1. Think about materials you could use for a texture weaving. Collect a variety of materials with a variety of textures, such as yarn, ribbon, leather, and wire.

2. Prepare a piece of cardboard for weaving by notching and stringing the warp threads.

3. Use a variety of textures in your weaving. Think about color variation as you weave.

Emphasis

Creative Expression

1. Find a picture of an athlete that can be imported into a blank paint or draw file, or scan a picture into a file.

2. Save the picture as a line drawing.

3. Use the paint tool to color in the athlete in bold, bright colors.

4. Color the rest of the picture, including the crowd, in neutral colors.

Activity Tips

Foreground, Middle Ground, and Background

🎨 Creative Expression

1. Think about details in your environment that you might include in your drawing.

2. Look through a viewing frame, and do two quick sketches of different areas. Choose one to make into a finished drawing.

3. Divide the picture plane on your paper into foreground, middle ground, and background. Begin by drawing the larger shapes of the foreground. Then fill in the middle ground and next the background. Finish by adding details to your foreground.

Perspective Techniques

🎨 Creative Expression

1. Think about the things you see in your environment every day.

2. Sketch several scenes you would like to draw. Include all six perspective techniques in your sketches.

3. Select your best sketch. Use chalk to draw the scene, and fill it with color. Remember to use all six perspective techniques to create the feeling of depth.

Activity Tips

Point of View

Creative Expression

1. Think about three-dimensional objects you would like to photograph. Select one.

2. Look carefully at the object you have chosen. Place it in front of you. Walk around it, stand above it, or lie on the ground and look at it. Choose and photograph your three favorite points of view.

Face Proportion Measurements

Creative Expression

1. Use a pencil to draw an egg shape for your head.

2. Draw a guideline from the top of the oval to the bottom. Find the center of the oval. Draw a horizontal line across the center. Divide each half one more time with light guidelines.

3. Sketch your eyes so that the center line goes through the center of your eyes. Be sure you have a space the width of one eye between the eyes. Follow the diagram on page 170 and continue looking in the mirror. Draw your nose, ears and hair, and neck.

4. Complete the drawing by using pastels to add color. Add interest to the background with a contrasting color.

Activity Tips

Unit 5 · Lesson 5　Body Proportions

🎨 Creative Expression

1. Study the model and setting using sighting to determine how the different parts relate to each other.

2. Place your seven and a half head lines so that your figure will fill the paper from top to bottom.

3. Sketch the figure using a light color crayon, such as yellow.

4. After the sketch is complete, fill the composition with color, texture, and value.

Unit 5 · Lesson 6　Distortion

🎨 Creative Expression

1. Insert a picture of yourself onto a blank photo editing file.

2. Convert the picture to a line drawing. Save your work.

3. Choose different areas of the face to stretch and distort. Try moving some features around. Save your work and print a copy.

4. Use a marker to divide the areas of the face into sections.

5. Color each section using a different color pencil.

Activity Tips

Unit 6 · Lesson 1 Formal Balance

🎨 Creative Expression

1. Curve a foam sheet and make a cylinder form twelve inches tall. Glue the cylinder and secure it with paper clips at the top and bottom.

2. Cut geometric or free-form shapes to represent yourself or a member of your family.

3. Add shapes to represent the eyes, nose, mouth, and hair. Use sizes, shapes, and colors to create exaggeration in the face.

4. Attach the face to your post. Use more shapes to create arms, legs, and other patterns on the post.

Unit 6 · Lesson 2 Informal Balance

🎨 Creative Expression

1. Think of the members of your family. Imagine a time when you are relaxing together. Where are the people sitting?

2. Use a pencil to lightly sketch the scene.

3. With watercolor crayons, fill in the large areas of your drawing.

4. Use water and a watercolor brush to blend the watercolor crayon.

5. After the painting dries, use markers to add the hair, eyes, eyebrows, lips and other details.

Activity Tips

Radial Balance

🎨 Creative Expression

1. Cross wooden craft sticks and glue them together. Glue the end of a piece of yarn behind the center of the sticks.

2. Hold the sticks so they look like an X. With the yarn hanging from the bottom, wrap it diagonally over the middle and then over the top right arm of the X.

3. Turn the X one clockwise turn to wrap each stick. As you wrap the yarn, make sure the rows of the yarn lie side by side. Continue to wrap until you see an "eye" forming at the center.

4. Tie the end of the last piece of yarn and tuck it under. Tie a loop of yarn on top for hanging your design.

Harmony

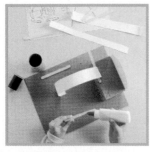

🎨 Creative Expression

1. Think of the type of sculpture that would fit the environment of your school. Choose an appropriate site for your sculpture.

2. Draw several sketches of how you want your sculpture to look. Select one sketch as your plan.

3. Using cardboard and found objects, build a model of your sculpture. Use analogous colors to create harmony in your design.

Activity Tips

Variety and Emphasis

🎨 Creative Expression

1. Select an animal image or images and develop a sketch. Add a background to the sketch.

2. Transfer the sketch to a large sheet of drawing paper and trace it with a black marker.

3. After your teacher demonstrates, color in the animal or animals using crayons to create textures.

4. Paint the entire background using watercolors in a color that contrasts with the color of the animal to create variety.

Unity

🎨 Creative Expression

1. Your teacher will give you a coil that has one end cut at an angle. Refer to the Coiled Basket Technique Tips to start wrapping the first row.

2. Continue wrapping the coil with fabric and making stitches on the first row about every five inches apart.

3. To make the sides of your coil basket, place one row of coiling on top of the previous row and stitch tightly. Continue adding rows of coiling.

4. To finish the basket, taper the end of the coil and lay it flat against the last row. Wrap your fabric tightly three times around the coil and cut the remaining fabric.

Visual Index

Artist Unknown
Egyptian Cat
716–332 B.C. (page 135)

Artist Unknown
Standing Ruler
c. A.D. 600–800. (page 130)

Artist Unknown
Jaguar
c. 1440–1521.
(page 134)

Andrea del Verrocchio
David
1473–1475. (page 172)

Michelangelo
Pietà
c. 1500. (page 124)

**Pieter Bruegel
(the Elder)**
Children's Games
1560. (page 44)

Paolo Veronese
Sheet of Studies for "The Martyrdom of Saint George"
1566. (page 41)

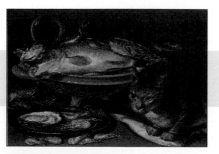

Clara Peeters
Still Life of Fish and Cat
after 1620. (page 113)

Peter Paul Rubens
The Meeting of David and Abigail
1625–1628. (page 147)

Judith Leyster
The Concert
c. 1631–1633. (page 184)

Rembrandt van Rijn
The Visitation
1640. (page 146)

Gu Mei
Orchids and Rocks
1644. (page 52)

John Singleton Copley
Sir William Pepperrell and His Family
1778. (page 154)

Katsushika Hokusai
Boy with a Flute
early 19th century.
(page 53)

William Johnson
Lovebird Token
early 19th century.
(page 195)

Artist Unknown
Figure from House Post
19th century. (page 186)

Joshua Johnson
The Westwood Children
c. 1807. (page 190)

Artist Unknown
Canister
1825. (page 105)

Artist Unknown
Yeihl Nax'in Raven Screen
c. 1830. (page 104)

Katsushika Hokusai
Winter Loneliness, from
One Hundred Poems
Explained by the Nurse
1839. (page 87)

Artist Unknown
Ceremonial Shield
c. 1852. (page 108)

James McNeill Whistler
Drouet
1859. (page 56)

Camille Pissarro
The Hermitage at Pontoise
1867. (page 156)

Martin Johnson Heade
Cattleya Orchid and Three
Brazilian Hummingbirds
1871. (page 203)

Pierre-Auguste Renoir
Portrait of a Young Boy
(Andre Berard)
1879. (page 168)

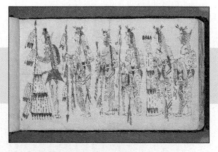

Chief Black Hawk
Crow Men in Ceremonial Dress
1880–1881. (page 78)

John Singer Sargent
The Daughters of Edward
Darley Boit
1882. (page 191)

Charles Edenshaw
Model Totem Pole
c. 1885. (page 187)

Berthe Morisot
Girl in a Boat with Geese
c. 1889. (page 157)

Paul Gauguin
Faaturuma (Melancholic)
1891. (page 120)

Artist Unknown
Basket
c. 1900. (page 207)

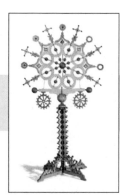

John Scholl
Sunburst
1907–1916. (page 194)

Vladimir Baranoff-Rossine
Symphony Number 1
1913. (page 198)

Marc Chagall
Paris Through the Window
1913. (page 177)

Natalya Goncharova
Maquillage
1913. (page 34)

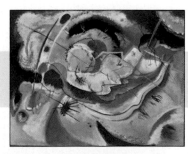

Wassily Kandinsky
*Little Painting with Yellow
(Improvisation)*
1914. (page 37)

Georgia O'Keeffe
Blue and Green Music
1919. (page 116)

Robert Henri
Bernadita
1922. (page 169)

Jacques Lipchitz
Reclining Figure with Guitar
1928. (page 127)

Georgia O'Keeffe
Yellow Hickory Leaves with Daisy
1928. (page 202)

Grant Wood
The Birthplace of Herbert Hoover, West Branch, Iowa
1931. (page 160)

Paul Klee
Mask of Fear
1932. (page 109)

Giorgio Morandi
Still Life with Coffee Pot
1933. (page 57)

Stuart Davis
Composition
1935. (page 64)

Barbara Hepworth
Three Forms
1935. (page 199)

Antonio Ruíz
The Bicycle Race
1938. (page 161)

Emily Carr
Self Portrait
1939. (page 60)

Henri Matisse
*Portrait of a Woman
with a Hood*
1939. (page 49)

Stuart Davis
Report from Rockport
1940. (page 97)

Z. Vanessa Helder
Rocks and Concrete
c. 1940. (page 101)

Joan Miró
*Symbols and Love
Constellations of a Woman*
1941. (page 79)

Richard Pousette-Dart
Within the Room
1942. (page 83)

Joaquín Torres-García
Abstract Art in Five Tones and Complementaries
1943. (page 67)

Lee Krasner
Milkweed
1955. (page 139)

Milton Avery
The White Wave
1956. (page 100)

Audrey Flack
Self Portrait (the Memory)
1958. (page 40)

Salvador Dalí
The Elephants (Design for the Opera la Dama Spagnola e il Cavaliere Romano)
1961. (page 176)

Wayne Thiebaud
Around the Cake
1962. (page 112)

Chryssa
Americanoom
1963. (page 142)

Teodora Blanco
Woman
1965. (page 131)

Minnie Evans
Design Made at
Airlie Gardens
1967. (page 70)

Henry Moore
Oval with Points
1968–1970. (page 126)

Eliot Elisofon
Asante Paramount Chief
Nana Akyanfuo Akowuah
Dateh II, Akwamuhene of
Kumase
1970. (page 75)

Paul Goodnight
Endangered Species
c. 1970. (page 45)

Jacob Lawrence
Study for the Munich Olympic
Games Poster
1971. (page 180)

Romare Bearden
Noah, Third Day
1972. (page 138)

Allan Houser
Coming of Age
1977. (page 86)

Leo Sewell
Stegosaurus
1984. (page 150)

Miriam Schapiro
Pas de Deux
1986. (page 94)

John Biggers
Shotguns, Fourth Ward
1987. (page 66)

John Biggers
Starry Crown
1987. (page 90)

Malcah Zeldis
Miss Liberty Celebration
1987. (page 117)

David Hockney
Large Interior Los Angeles
1988. (page 96)

Jaune Quick-to-See Smith
Rainbow
1989. (page 36)

Duane Hanson
High School Student
1990. (page 173)

Benny Andrews
Patriots
1991. (page 48)

Michael Naranjo
Eagle's Song
1992. (page 164)

Michael Naranjo
Eagle's Song
1992. (page 165)

Sandy Skoglund
The Cocktail Party
1992. (page 142)

Patssi Valdez
The Magic Room
1994. (page 82)

Viola Frey
Family Portrait
1995. (page 210)

Elizabeth Murray
Riverbank
1997. (page 71)

Carolyn Mazloomi
Mask Communion
1998. (page 74)

Mary A. Jackson
Low Basket with Handle
1999. (page 206)

Glossary

Pronunciation Key: at; l**ā**te; c**â**re; f**ä**ther; s**e**t; m**ē**; **i**t; k**ī**te; **o**x r**ō**se; **ô** in b**ou**ght; **c**oin; b**oo**k; t**oo**; f**o**rm; **ou**t; **u**p; **ū**se; t**û**rn; **ə** sound in **a**bout, chick**e**n, penc**i**l, cann**o**n, circ**u**s, **ch**air; **hw** in **wh**ich; ri**ng**; **sh**op; **th**in; **th**ere; **zh** in trea**s**ure.

A

additive sculpture (ad′ i tiv skulp′ chər), *noun* When something is added to either relief or freestanding sculpture

alternating pattern (ôl′ tər nāt ing pat′ ərn), *noun* Can repeat a motif, but change position; alter spacing between motifs or add a second motif

analogous color scheme (ə nal′ ə gəs kul′ ər skēm′), *noun* Uses colors that are side by side on the color wheel and have a common color

ant's view (ants′ vu′), *noun* Viewers feel they are looking up, toward an object or figure.

assemblage (ä säm bläzh′), *noun* A sculpture technique in which a variety of objects is assembled to create one complete piece

asymmetry (ā sim′ i trē), *noun* Another name for informal balance

B

background (bak′ ground′), *noun* The area of the picture plane farthest from the viewer

balance (bal′ əns), *noun* The principle of design that deals with visual weight in an artwork

bird's-eye view (bûrdz ī vu′), *noun* Or aerial view; viewers feel they are looking down on a scene.

blending (blen ding), *noun* A shading technique that creates a gradual change from light to dark or dark to light

blind contour drawing (blīnd′ kon′ tūr drô′ ing), *noun* A drawing that is made by looking at the object being drawn, not at the paper.

body proportions (bod′ ē prə pôr shənz), *noun* The size relationship of one part of the body to another

C

central axis (sen′ trəl ak′ sis), *noun* A real or imaginary dividing line which can run in two directions, vertically and horizontally

close-up view (klos′ up vu′), *noun* Viewers feel they are right next to an object, or are a part of the action in a picture.

collage (kō läzh), *noun* A two-dimensional work of art made up of pieces of paper and/or fabric to create the image.

color (kul' ər), *noun* 1. The art element that is created from reflected light; 2. In balance: a brighter color has more visual weight than a dull color; 3. In perspective: bright-colored objects seem closer, while dull or pale objects appear farther away.

color scheme (kul' ər skēm'), *noun* A plan for organizing the colors used in an artwork

color spectrum (kul' ər spek' trum), *noun* A band of colors in the order of red, orange, yellow, green, blue, and violet

color wheel (kul' ər 'wēl), *noun* Shows the color spectrum bent into a circle

complementary color scheme (kom' plə men tə rē kul' ər skēm'), *noun* Uses one set of complementary colors; for example, red and green, blue and orange, and yellow and violet

complementary colors (kom' plə men tə rē kul' ərz), *noun* Colors that are opposite each other on the color wheel

contour (kon' tür), *noun* The edges and surface ridges of an object

contour hatching (kon' tür hach' ing), *noun* A shading technique that follows the form of an object

contour line (kon' tür līn), *noun* Defines the edges and surface ridges of an object

contrast (kon' trast), *noun* 1. Difference; 2. A technique for creating a focal point or area of interest in a work of art using differences in elements; 3. In emphasis: contrast occurs when one element stands out from the rest of the work.

cool colors (kül kul' erz), *noun* Green, violet, and blue. They suggest coolness and move away from the viewer.

cross-hatching (krôs hach' ing), *noun* A shading technique created when sets of parallel lines cross or intersect

curved (kûrvd), *adj.* A line that bends and changes gradually or turns inward to form spirals

D

dark lines (dark līnz), *noun* Created by using less water for watercolor paints

detail (dē tāl), *noun* One of the six perspective techniques. Objects with fuzzy, blurred edges appear farther away than those with clear sharp edges.

diagonal (dī ag' ə nəl), *noun (adj)* A line that moves on a slant

distortion (di stôr shən), *noun* A deviation from normal or expected proportions

dominant element (dom' ə nənt el' ə mənt), *noun* The element in a work of art that is noticed first.

E

emphasis (em' fə sis), *noun* The principle of design that stresses one area in an art work over another area

exaggeration (eg zaj' ə rā' shən), *noun* To increase or enlarge beyond what is expected or normal

F

face proportions (fas' prə pôr shənz), *noun* The relationship of one feature of a face to another feature

faraway view (fär' ə wa' vu'), *noun* Or eye-level view; viewers feel they are standing far away from the scene.

flowing lines (flō ing līnz), *noun* Create a feeling of calm and gracefulness. Flowing lines are fluid; they change direction and size.

flowing rhythm (flō ing rith' əm), *noun* Created when curved lines or shapes are repeated

focal point (fo' kəl point'), *noun* The point which the receding lines meet. It is the first part of a composition to attract the viewer's attention.

foreground (fôr' ground'), *noun* The area of the picture plane that is closest to the viewer

form (form), *noun* A three-dimensional object that is measured by height, width, and depth

formal balance (fôr' mel bal' əns), *noun* Occurs when equal or similar elements are placed on opposite sides of a central axis

free-form forms (frē' fôrm' fôrmz), *noun* Three-dimensional forms with irregular edges often found in nature

free-form shapes (frē' fôrm' shāps), *noun* Two-dimensional images made of straight or curved lines or a combination of both

freestanding sculpture (frē stan' ding skulp chər), *noun* A type of sculpture that is surrounded by space on all sides.

G

geometric forms (je' ə met' rik fôrmz), *noun* Mathematically precise forms based on geometric shapes

geometric shapes (je' ə met' rik shāps), *noun* Mathematically precise shapes: circle, square, and triangle

gesture (jes' chər), *noun* An expressive movement

gesture lines (jes' chər līnz), *noun* Lines drawn to capture the movement of a person, an animal, or an object in a painting or drawing

gesture sketch (jes' chər skech), *noun* Quick drawings used to capture the position or pose of the body

H

harmony (här′ mə nē), *noun*   The principle of art which creates unity by stressing similarities of separate but related parts

hatching (hach′ ing), *noun*   A shading technique that looks like a series of parallel lines

horizontal (hôr′ ə zon təl), *noun*   Lines that move from side to side

hue (hū), *noun*   Another name for color

I

informal balance (in fôr′məl bal′ əns), *noun*   A way of organizing parts of a design so that unlike objects have equal visual weight

intensity (in ten′ si te), *noun*   The brightness or dullness of a color

intermediate colors (in′ tər m′ de it kul′ ərs), *noun*   Yellow-green, red-orange, blue-green; made by combining a primary with either of the secondary colors that are adjacent on the color wheel

invented texture (in ven′ təd teks′ chər), *noun*   Created when an artist uses lines or other elements to make a textural look without any specific texture in mind

isolation (ī′ sə lā′ shən), *noun*   An object is emphasized by its placement apart from other objects.

L

light lines (līt līnz), *noun*   Created by adding more water to watercolor paints

line (līn), *noun*   A mark drawn by a tool such as a pencil, pen, or paintbrush as it moves across a surface

lines (līnz), *noun*   One of the six perspective techniques. Parallel lines seem to converge or move toward the same point as they move away from you.

location (lō cā′ shən), *noun*   Artists can emphasize an object by placing it closer to the center of the piece.

M

matte (mat), *noun*   A dull, sometimes rough finish

middle ground (mid′ əl ground′), *noun*   The area of the picture plane that is usually toward the center

minimal details (min ə məl dē tāl), *noun*   Used in gesture sketches to complete the drawing

mix a neutral color (miks ā nü trəl kul′ ər), *noun*   Mix a neutral color with another color to change its value

mixed-media (mikst mē dē′ ə), *noun*   An art object that has been created from an assortment of media or materials

monochromatic (mon′ ə kro mat′ ik), *adj.*   A color scheme that is made up of one color and the tints and shade of that color

monochromatic color scheme
(mon' ə kro mat' ik kul' ər skēm'),
noun   Uses only one color and the
values of that color

motif (mō tēf), *noun*   A unit that is
made up of objects or art elements
which is repeated

N

negative space (neg' ə tiv spas'),
noun   The empty space that sur-
rounds objects, shapes, and forms

neutral color scheme (nü trəl kul'
ər skēm'), *noun*   Uses black, white,
and a variety of grays

neutral colors (nü trəl kul' ərz),
noun   Black, white, and gray

nonobjective (non' əb jek' tiv), *adj.*
Art that has no recognizable subject
matter

O

overlapping (o' vər lap ing), *noun*
1. One object covers a portion of
another object. 2. In perspective:
one of the six perspective techniques; the object covering another
will appear closer to the viewer, creating a feeling of depth.

P

parallel lines (per ə lel līnz), *noun*
Lines that move in the same direction and always stay the same
distance apart

pattern (pat' ərn), *noun*
A repeated surface decoration

perspective techniques (pər spek'
tiv tek neks'), *noun*   The six techniques an artist uses to create the
illusion of depth in two-dimensional
art: overlapping, size, placement,
detail, color, converging lines

picture plane (pik' chər plān'),
noun   The surface of a drawing or
painting

placement (plās ment), *noun*   One
of the six perspective techniques.
Objects placed lower in the picture
plane appear to be closer than those
placed near eye level. There are
three areas on a picture plane: foreground, middle ground, and background.

point of view (point' əv vū), *noun*
The angle at which the viewer sees
an object

portrait (por trət), *noun*   A two or
three-dimensional artwork created
in the image of a person or animal

position (pə zish' ən), *noun*   In
balance: a larger, positive shape and
a small, negative space can be balanced by a small, positive shape and
a large, negative space.

positive space (poz' i tiv spas'),
noun   Refers to any object, shape,
or form in two- and three-
dimensional art

primary colors (pri' mer ē kul' ərs),
noun   Red, yellow, and blue, used
to mix the other colors on the color
wheel

profile (prō fīl), *noun*   A side view
of a person or animal

proportion (prə pôr' shən), *noun* The principle of art that is concerned with the size relationship of one part to another

R

radial balance (rā' dē əl bal' əns), *noun* A type of balance that occurs when the art elements come out, or radiate, from a central point

random pattern (ran' dəm pat' ərn), *noun* Occurs when the motif is repeated in no apparent order

regular pattern (reg' yə lər pat' ərn), *noun* Occurs when identical motifs are repeated with an equal amount of space between them

relief sculpture (ri lēf skulp chər), *noun* A type of sculpture that has objects that stick out from a flat surface.

repeated lines (rē pō təd līnz), *noun* Used to give the feeling of movement or motion in a gesture drawing

repeated shapes (rē pē təd shāps), *noun* Used to give the feeling of movement or motion in a gesture drawing; the more times a shape is repeated, the faster the motion looks.

rough (rəf), *noun* A surface that has ridges; not smooth

S

secondary colors (sek' ən der' ē kul' ərs), *noun* Oorange, green and violet; the result of mixing two primary colors

self-portrait (self por trət), *noun* A two or three-dimensional artwork that an artist makes of him or herself

sets of complementary colors (set əf kom' plə men tə rē kul' ərz), *noun* There are three sets on the color wheel: red and green, blue and orange, and yellow and violet.

shade (shād), *noun* Any color blended with black

shading (shā ding), *noun* A technique for creating dark values or darkening an area by repeating marks such as lines or dots

shape (shāp) *noun* A two-dimensional area that is measured by height and width

silhouette (sil' ü et') *noun* The shape of a shadow

shiny (shī nē), *noun* Bright from reflected light

simulated texture (sim' u la' təd teks chər), *noun* Imitates real textures, see also visual texture

size (sīz), *noun* 1. In perspective: objects that are closer look larger than objects that are farther away; 2. In balance: a large shape or form will appear to be heavier than a small shape, and several small shapes can balance one large shape.

space (spās), *noun*   The art element that refers to the areas above, below, between, within, and around an object

spectral color scheme (spek trəl kul' ər skēm'), *noun*   Uses all the colors of the rainbow: red, orange, yellow, green, blue, and violet

smooth (smüth), *noun*   A surface free from roughness; even

still life (stil' līf'), *noun*   The arrangement of common inanimate objects from which artists draw or paint

subtractive sculpture (sub trak tiv skulp chər), *noun*   When an artist carves pieces away from a form

symmetry (sim' i trē), *noun*   A type of formal balance in which two halves of a balanced artwork are identical, mirror images of each other

T

tactile texture (tak' təl teks' chər), *noun*   Actual texture, texture that can really be felt

texture (teks' chər), *noun*   1. The art element that refers to the way something feels; 2. In balance: a rough texture has an uneven pattern of highlights and shadows. For this reason, a rough surface attracts the viewer's eyes more easily than a smooth, even surface.

thick line (thik līn), *noun*   Created by beginning with a thin line and gradually pressing the brush down

thin line (thin līn), *noun*   Created when a brush is held vertically to paper and touched lightly with the tip of the brush

tint (tint), *noun*   any color blended with white

two-dimensional (tü' di men' shən nəl), *adj.*   Flat; can only be measured by height and length

U

unity (ū' ni tē), *noun*   The feeling of wholeness or oneness that is achieved by properly using the elements and principles in art

V

value (val' ū), *noun*   The lightness or darkness of a color

variety (və ri' ə tē), *noun*   The principle of art which is concerned with difference or contrast

vertical (vür' tə kəl), *noun*   A line that moves from top to bottom

visual movement (vizh' ü əl müv' mənt), *noun*   Occurs when the eye is pulled through a work of art by of rhythm of beats and rests

visual rhythm (vizh' ü əl rith' əm), *noun*   The principle of design that organizes the elements in a work of art by repeating elements and/or objects

visual texture (vizh′ ü əl teks′ chər), *noun* Or simulated texture, imitates real texture. It is the illusion of a three-dimensional surface.

visual weight (vizh′ ü əl wāt), *noun* cannot be measured on a scale; it is measured by which objects the viewer's eyes see first.

W

warm colors (wōrm′ kul′ ərz), *noun* Red, yellow, and orange. They suggest warmth and come forward toward the viewer.

Z

zigzag (zig′ zag) *noun (adj.)* A line that is made by joining diagonal lines

Index

Photo Credits

Cover Alfred Stieglitz Collection, gift of Georgia O'Keeffe, 1969.835. Image © The Art Institute of Chicago. © 2004 The Georgia O'Keeffe Foundation/Artists Rights Society (ARS), New York; 5 Dallas Museum of Art, Dallas, Texas; 6 Smithsonian American Art Museum/Art Resource, NY. © Estate of Stuart Davis/Licensed by VAGA, New York, New York; 7 Steinbaum Krauss Gallery, New York; 8 © Scala/Art Resource, NY/ St. Peter's Basilica, Vatican State; 9 North Carolina Museum of Art. Purchased with funds from the State of North Carolina; 10 National Museum of Women in the Arts. Washington, DC; 12 (tl) Museum of Fine Arts, Boston, (tr) Hirshhorn Museum and Sculpture Garden, Smithsonian Institution, Gift of Joseph H. Hirshhorn, 1966, (bl) Dallas Museum of Art, Dallas, Texas, (br) © Philip Hayson/Photo Researchers Inc; 13 (tl) Honolulu Academy of Art. Honolulu, Hawaii. Gift of James A. Michener, 1955 (13,694), (tr) Purchased with funds provided by the Smithsonian Collections Acquisition Program. Photograph by Frank Khoury. National Museum of African Art, Smithsonian Institution, Washington D.C., (bl) Image no.EEPA 1474. Eliot Elisofon Photographic Archives, National Museum of African Art, Smithsonian Institution, Washington, D.C., (br) Royal British Columbia Museum, Victoria, Canada; 15 (tl) The Ogden Museum of Southern Art, University of New Orleans, Gift of the Benny Andrews Foundation, (tr) Amon Carter Museum, Fort Worth, Texas. 1999.33.E, (bl) From the Girard Foundation Collection, in the Museum of International Folk Art, a unit of the Museum of New Mexico, Santa Fe, New Mexico. Photographer: Michel Monteaux, (br) © Carl & Ann Purcell/Corbis; 16 Helen Birch Bartlett Memorial Collection, 1926.252. Photograph © 2001, The Art Institute of Chicago, All Rights Reserved; 17 © Northwest Museum of Arts & Culture. Photo by David Anderson; 18 Wadsworth Atheneum, Hartford. The Ella Gallup Sumner and Mary Catlin Sumner Collection Fund; 19 (t) Dallas Museum of Art, Dallas, Texas, (b) Smithsonian American Art Museum, Washington, DC/Art Resource, NY. © Elizabeth Catlett/Licensed By VAGA, New York, New York; 20 National Gallery, London/Art Resource, NY. Erich Lessing, photographer; 21 Frank Fortune; 22 (t, tcl, tcr, br, bcr) © Photodisc/Getty Images, Inc, (bcl, bl) © Digital Vision/Getty Images, Inc; 23 (t) © Corbis, (tcl, tcr, bl, bcl, bc)© Photodisc/Getty Images, Inc, (br) © Index Stock; 24, 26, 28, 30 San Francisco Museum of Modern Art. © Banco de Mexico Diego Rivera & Frida Kahlo Museum Trust. Av. Cinco de Mayo No.2, Col. Centro, Del. Cuauhtemoc 06059, Mexico, D.F; 32-33 © Aaron Haupt; 34 Dallas Museum of Art, Dallas, Texas. © 2004 Artists Rights Society (ARS), New York/ADAGP, Paris; 35 © Tretyakov Gallery, Moscow, Russia/Bridgeman Art Library; 36 Steinbaum Krauss Gallery; 37 Philadelphia Museum of Art: The Louis and Walter Arensberg Collection. 1950-134-103. © 2004 Artists Rights Society (ARS), New York/ADAGP, Paris; 38 © Eclipse Studios; 39 Frank Fortune; 40 Miami University Art Museum, Oxford, Ohio; 41 Courtesy of the J. Paul Getty Museum; 42 © Eclipse Studios; 43 Randy Ellett; 44 Photograph © Erich Lessing/Art Resource, NY; 45 Courtesy of Bing Davis; 46 © Eclipse Studios; 47 Randy Ellett; 48 Cumberland Gallery, Nashville, TN; 49 The Bridgeman Art Library; 50 © Eclipse Studios; 51 Randy Ellett; 52 Arthur M. Sackler Gallery, Smithsonian Institution; 53 Freer Gallery, Smithsonian Institution; 54 © Eclipse Studios; 55 Randy Ellett; 56 Los Angeles County Museum of Art, The Julius L. and Anita Zelman Collection. Photo © 2003 Museum Associates/LACMA; 57 © Bettmann/Corbis, © 2004 Artists Rights Society (ARS), New York/SIAE, Rome; 58 © Eclipse Studios; 59 Randy Ellett; 60 © National Gallery of Canada, Ottawa. Gift of Peter Bronfman, 1990; 62 Courtesy of the Wadsworth Atheneum, Hartford, CN; 63 Craig Schwartz; 64 Smithsonian American Art Museum/Art Resource, NY. © Estate of Stuart Davis/Licensed by VAGA, New York, New York; 65 © Ralph Morse/Getty Images; 66 Hampton University Museum; 67 Collection Albright-Knox Art Gallery, Buffalo, New York. Gift of Mr. and Mrs. Armand J. Castellani, 1979. © 2004 Artists Rights Society (ARS), New York/VEGAP, Madrid; 68 © Eclipse Studios; 69 Frank Fortune; 70 Smithsonian American Art Museum/Art Resource, NY; 71 Collection Albright-Knox Art Gallery Buffalo, New York. Sarah Norton Goodyear Fund, 1997; 72 © Eclipse Studios; 73 Randy Ellett; 74 Frank Fortune; 75 Image no.EEPA 1474. Eliot Elisofon Photographic Archives, National Museum of African Art, Smithsonian Institution, Washington, D.C; 76 Eclipse Studios; 77 Randy Ellett; 78 Thaw Collection Fenimore House Museum/NYSHA, Cooperstown, New York. Photo © 1998 by; 79 The Art Institute of Chicago. Gift of Gilbert W. Chapman. © 2004 Succession Miro/Artists Rights Society (ARS), New York/ADAGP, Paris; 80 Eclipse Studio; 81 Randy Ellett; 82 © Smithsonian American Art Museum, Washington, DC/Art Resource, NY; 83 Collection of the Whitney Museum of American Art, New York. Promised 50th Anniversary Gift of the Artist; 84 © Eclipse Studios; 85 Frank Fortune; 86 Denver Art Museum; 87 Honolulu Academy of Art. Honolulu, Hawaii. Gift of James A. Michener, 1955 (13,694); 88 © Eclipse Studios; 89 Frank Fortune; 90 Dallas Museum of Art, Dallas, Texas; 92 The Image Bank/Getty Images, Inc; 93 Allen Nomura; 94 Steinbaum Krauss Gallery, New York; 95 © Suzanne Opton/Courtesy Steinbaum Krauss Gallery; 96 The Metropolitan Museum of Art, Purchase, Natasha Gelman Gift, in honor of William S. Lieberman, 1989. (1989.279) Photograph © 1990 The Metropolitan Museum of Art. © David Hockney; 97 The Metropolitan Museum of Art, Edith and Milton Lowenthal Collection, Bequest of Edith Abrahamson Lowenthal, 1991. (1992.24.1) Photograph © 1992 The Metropolitan Museum of Art. © Estate of Stuart Davis/Licensed by VAGA, New York, New York; 98 © Eclipse Studios; 99 Alexis Lee; 100 Gift of Helen Hooker Roelofs in memory of her father, Elon Huntington Hooker, Class of 1896. Courtesy of the Herbert F. Johnson Museum of Art, Cornell University. © 2004 Milton Avery Trust/Artists Rights Society (ARS), New York; 101 © Northwest Museum of Arts & Culture. Photo by David Anderson; 102 © Eclipse Studios; 103 Randy Ellett; 104 The Seattle Art Museum, Gift of John H. Haulberg. Photo by Paul Macapia; 105 Collection of the American Folk Art Museum, New York; Gift of the Historical Society of Early American Decoration; 106 © Eclipse Studios; 107 Randy Ellett; 108 The Brooklyn Museum, Brooklyn, New York. Frank L. Babbott and Carl H. DeSilver Funds; 109 © Digital image The Museum of Modern Art/Licensed by Scala/Art Resource, NY. © 2004 Artists Rights Society (ARS), New York/ADAGP, Paris; 110 © Eclipse Studios; 111 Frank Fortune; 112 © Wayne Thiebaud/Licensed by VAGA, New York, New York; 113 National Museum of Women in the Arts, Washington D.C; 114 © Eclipse Studios; 115 Frank Fortune; 116 Alfred Stieglitz